Last Boy of '66

Last Boy of '66

MY STORY OF ENGLAND'S
WORLD CUP WINNING TEAM

GEOFF
HURST

WITH JASPER REES

**EBURY
SPOTLIGHT**

Ebury Spotlight, an imprint of Ebury Publishing
One Embassy Gardens, 8 Viaduct Gdns,
Nine Elms, London SW11 7BW

Ebury Spotlight is part of the Penguin Random House
group of companies whose addresses can be found at
global.penguinrandomhouse.com

First published by Ebury Spotlight in 2024

www.penguin.co.uk

A CIP catalogue record for this book is available from the British Library

ISBN 9781529938487

Printed and bound in Great Britain by Clays Ltd, Elcograf S.p.A.

Imported into the EEA by Penguin Random House Ireland, Morrison Chambers,
32 Nassau Street, Dublin D02 YH68

Penguin Random House is committed to a sustainable future
for our business, our readers and our planet. This book is
made from Forest Stewardship Council® certified paper.

To our darling Claire and the Boys of '66

Contents

1

IT WAS THEN

I am sitting in a café when a text comes through from my granddaughter Grace. She has a question for me.

'Were u still playing for West Ham when u did the World Cup final?'

Grace is 15 and she's working on a project at school. The brief is to interview an adult about a key event in their life, to ask a series of detailed questions about the impact it has had on them. She's already put most of these to me face to face. It was quite a grilling. But now she's after a bit more background information. Some facts.

'Yes,' I text back.

Grace knows something about the big event in my life, but it's hardly her fault that she's unfamiliar with a few of the basics. I have been blessed with five grandchildren. At the time of writing they range from 35 all the way down to seven. Despite that considerable age span, I hope there's one thing they would all agree on: their grandpa doesn't spend his precious time with them bending their ear with tales of yester-year from before they were born. Or in Grace's case, from long before her mother was born.

But yes, I did play for West Ham United back then. Famously, so did a couple of my teammates on that historic day.

3

It was Hammers who scored the goals. All four of them. Another Hammer – the very best of us – set up the first and the last.

West Ham 4 West Germany 2.

Another text arrives.

'And who asked u to play for the England team? Or how did u get on the England team?'

'Alf Ramsey,' I reply. 'Alf Ramsey picked me.'

Many people know these things. They know that Alf Ramsey was knighted for his achievement. They know he sent out a team that was dubbed the Wingless Wonders, and in their sleep they can reel off the names of those 11 players. But there are younger generations who, even if they know who managed England, don't know much more. About his vision, his drive, his loyalty. Also his shyness, even awkwardness, and his unease with the press.

Alf – he was always formal with us, and yet he wanted all his players to call him Alf – lost his job as England manager 50 years ago, in 1974, after a freak result at Wembley against Poland that meant England failed for the first time to qualify for the World Cup finals. 'We've got the bastard,' one journalist is said to have crowed in the press box that night. But anybody who knows anything about football in England knows this: that no one who has succeeded him in the job has matched his achievement. Most haven't even got close. Bobby Robson got to a quarter-final and a semi. So did Gareth Southgate. Sven-Göran Eriksson reached the last eight twice. Glenn Hoddle and Fabio Capello made it to the round of 16. Roy Hodgson didn't make it out of the group. Don Revie and Graham Taylor did not qualify.

I promise I'm not remotely gloating when I write these words. It gives me no pleasure to dwell on the national team's underachievement. Hand on heart, I have been very disappointed over the years. 'You won it once,' Alf famously said to us on the pitch between full time and extra time. 'Now go and win it again.' But England never have. I'm an Englishman and an England fan and I would love nothing more. I was even part of a coaching team that had a crack at it.

'OK thank u,' texts Grace. 'Did u coach on the England team?'

'Yes I was assistant to Ron Greenwood, 1977–1982.' I could have added that the first day I reported for duty coincided with the christening of Grace's mum. We had to move it from the afternoon to the morning so I could get to the church.

History relates that in Spain in 1982, thanks to an experimental format devised by FIFA, my old West Ham manager made it to the last 12. This was the first World Cup England had competed in for a dozen years. I was on the pitch in Mexico for the last game we had played in the tournament, the quarter-final in 1970 where we were two-up against West Germany in León and then they scored three. Yes, that game. Now I was part of the coaching team.

Not for the last time, we travelled to Spain with our best player injured. Kevin Keegan didn't make it onto the pitch until our fifth game, the one we were knocked out in. Such absences would become a regular thing. You could set your watch by them. See also Bryan Robson in 1986, David Beckham in 2002, Wayne Rooney in 2006.

At the time, all these injuries became a national obsession. Would England's talisman be ready in time? Would Captain Fantastic's smashed metatarsal or twanged tendon or tweaked eyelash heal by the knockout stage? Every time it happened, the back pages could barely focus on anything else, and often the front pages joined in too.

But no injury to an England player had quite the impact of the gash sustained by Jimmy Greaves in 1966. In the third group game the studs of a Frenchman penetrated his shin to the bone. It was a split second that changed the path of Jimmy's life. It also changed mine. Jimmy needed stitches and Alf needed a forward to replace him. Crazy though it might now seem, there were only three forwards in the entire 22-man squad. Roger Hunt was already in the team. Jimmy was now injured. The spare striker, watching the group games in a grey suit issued by the Football Association, was me.

'And here comes Hurst,' said Kenneth Wolstenholme in English football's most memorable burst of commentary. 'He's got …'

Jimmy's injury seemed to close a door on a destiny that felt pre-written. He was the greatest goalscorer in England's history. He was a shoo-in, every time. I don't mind admitting that he was the better player, by a distance.

'Some people are on the pitch!'

If England were going to get to the World Cup final, no one could imagine them doing it without him. He was a genius of the penalty box.

'They think it's all over!'

But he wasn't available for the quarter-final. I was given my chance, and I seized it.

'It is now.'

Ever since, it could be argued, I have lived a life that might have been Jimmy's.

As for the impact of 30 July 1966, Grace has plenty of questions on that. The questionnaire falls under five main headings: Physical, Intellectual, Emotional, Social, Financial. Not all of them seem relevant to playing international football at the highest level. 'Have you lost weight from this event?' 'Did this event impact on your ability to perform certain skills?' But others hit the target. 'Did you experience new opportunities from this event?' 'Would you be able to provide some more information about the emotional impact on you?' 'Did this event affect your relationship with your family?' 'Have you gone through a change in wealth due to this event?' Some require me to reflect on how I felt about the sad times in my life.

Grace must be the first person who doesn't utter the most frequently asked question of all.

Was it really a goal?

I keep my answers reasonably brief because she surely doesn't need pages and pages about my life for a school project. But if you do happen to be reading, Grace, the following pages contain some longer answers.

This isn't the first book with my name on the cover. There was a biography written soon after the World Cup. I did a longer memoir in 2001, many years after I had left football for good. But I was not ready to dig as deep as I find I want to now as I advance through my ninth decade.

There have been unbelievable highs in my life, but there have also been lows. The deaths of my younger brother Robert and of my oldest daughter Claire are sadnesses that have taken decades to process. Footballers of my generation were no different from anyone else born in the 1940s. We were not encouraged or perhaps even allowed to talk about our feelings. So grief remained buried or unexpressed.

Meanwhile over the years there have been other departures.

Banksy, George, Jack, Mooro, Ray, Nobby, Bally, Bobby, Martin, Roger. My ten teammates. My old friends. The 11 of us shared in something that no other Englishman has ever experienced. Now they've all gone, heroes from an era that is slipping into sepia. The last of them to leave was Bobby Charlton. He died in October 2023 and suddenly I became the only survivor of a team who walked up the 39 steps to accept a winner's medal from Her Majesty the Queen. To be left to live on without them feels lonely – lonelier, in fact, than I can possibly put into words.

Last year, I was given a book by my wife Judith, who knows I'm not a big reader but couldn't resist getting this one for me when she saw it in a bookshop. *Answered Prayers: England and the 1966 World Cup* by Duncan Hamilton was published only weeks before Sir Bobby breathed his last. It's a fascinating tribute to Sir Alf, even though it's frank about what a complicated man he could be. The book's conclusion is that the FA didn't fully understand what it had in the England team that won the World Cup. A legacy was squandered, its heroes went uncelebrated. I'll absolutely go along with that. Fans never forgot us. The FA did.

But it was a sentence on the very last page that really grabbed me by the lapels.

'I think, rather pessimistically, that 1966 will fully regain its lustre and significance for us only on the day when there ceases to be anyone left who played in it.'

It's going to happen one day. There's no avoiding that final whistle. But it isn't all over, not yet. For now, one of us is still here.

And before I go, I want to get down my final thoughts about 1966 and all that. I want to talk about Alf. I want to talk about my teammates. I want to talk about Jimmy, the 12th man of whom there is no photograph in the iconic red shirt we wore that day. I want to talk about victory, but also I want to talk about loss.

Before diving in, I need to be up front about two things.

One is my memory. I've been reliving that big day ever since it happened, and some may feel they've heard the stories before. In my old age I have tried to think about those familiar tales in a fresh way, to dig below the surface and reflect on their significance. But because we're talking about events that happened up to 60 years ago, my recollection isn't always what it was. Don't worry, I have none of the symptoms of the dementia that cruelly ravaged some of my teammates. Or I don't think I have! My memory losses feel normal for my age, and proportionate. All the same, to remind myself of one or two details that have grown hazy with time, I've had a root around in my scrapbooks.

These were lovingly put together over the course of my whole career by my father-in-law. Here are matchday reports from my early days in football when I was described as 'big, strong and goal-conscious' or 'almost arrogant' or – my favourite – 'thrustful'. There are no fewer than six different clippings from the day of triumph when West Ham beat Man U 3–0. One scrapbook covers my older and wiser years in the red and white stripes of Stoke City. In 1996 a headline in the *Essex Chronicle* screams, LET'S HONOUR HERO HURST. It sounds as if they're putting me up for a knighthood – at that point I was an MBE. But no. It's a local newspaper campaign to award me freedom of the borough of Chelmsford. I haven't looked at any of this in decades, and here it all is, a comprehensive memory bank of yellowing cuttings.

I've also dived into the memoirs and biographies of my 1966 teammates to fill in some of the blanks of their lives and careers. In a sense they are my collaborators as I revisit our collective story. It's a wonderful way to enjoy their company again, to get us all together one last time. I was amazed to discover from one book that, as a kid on the training pitch at Blackpool, little Alan Ball (b. 1945) had the nerve to berate Stanley Matthews (b. 1915) for not running on to a pass of his. Classic Bally: he had the highest voice, but also the loudest. And absolutely no respect for his elders.

So that's the first thing. The other thing comes from a conversation with my wife. Judith has insisted that there mustn't be too much in the way of bad language. As a girl growing up in Chelmsford in the 1950s she never heard anyone swear. 'When I went into London,' she reminds me, 'and heard someone saying "bleeding", I thought it was the worst word I'd heard in my life.' She's caught up since, but tells me I've got a clean-cut image to maintain, nurtured over many years in the public eye. I was made a 'sir' just two years after the campaign to give me the freedom of Chelmsford, and knights are meant to speak the King's English. But when footballers get together it's not like a convocation of bishops. We speak the people's Anglo-Saxon. All of us, that is, apart from Sir Bobby Charlton. As Judith puts it ever so well, Bobby never put a foot wrong on the pitch or off it. His brother Jack, on the other hand, turned the air blue wherever he went.

So I'll do my best to keep it clean. But please excuse a little bit of effing and Geoffing from the last boy of '66.

2

RECAP

It was a long time ago now. To refresh the memory of anyone who is hazy about how the World Cup in 1966 unfolded, I thought it worthwhile to start with a brief history of England's progress through the tournament.

England were drawn in Group 1 with Uruguay, Mexico and France. Uruguay were our most dangerous opponents and, although it wasn't very entertaining to watch England bash their heads against a brick wall of a defence, both sides were satisfied to emerge from the opening game with a goalless draw. This was the first time England had failed to score at Wembley since 1938. England then took on Mexico. The game is memorable for Bobby Charlton's iconic wondergoal, a piledriver unleashed from 30 yards out that flew into the top-left corner. Roger Hunt scored a tap-in to make it 2–0. He then scored two against France for another 2–0 win.

I didn't play in any of the group games. But owing to the injury to Jimmy Greaves, I was called up for the quarter-final against Argentina. It was a brutal encounter in which we faced the kind of foul play that most of us had never experienced before. In the first half, after endlessly arguing with the referee, the Argentine captain Antonio Rattín became the first player ever to be sent off in an international at Wembley, though he took seven minutes to accept the verdict and actually leave the pitch. Even against ten men it was difficult to break them down, but eventually I darted to the near post to get my head on the end of a Martin Peters cross and we won by the game's only goal.

The semi-final was against Portugal, who were thought to be the best side left in the competition. They were led by the great Eusébio, but Nobby Stiles marked him out of the game. Bobby Charlton scored both our goals: one was a brilliant low sidefooted drive from outside the box after the goalkeeper's half-clearance; the other was another thunderbolt, which I teed up for him by getting on to the end of a long ball into the box. A late penalty from Eusébio, after Jack Charlton handballed a goal-bound header, made it 2–1. Coming at the very end of the fifth game, it was the first goal England had conceded in the tournament.

Then came the final.

3

LESS IS MOORO

With no one in the world of football do I go back further than Bobby Moore. We played many hundreds of games together. For ten years at West Ham United, from 1962 to 1972, he was at the back and I was up front. Then there are my England caps. Over the course of six of those years, I was picked to represent my country 49 times and he was my captain all the way through. He was playing for England before I started, and still playing for them after I finished. Two of my goals on the famous, fateful day – the first and the third – were created by Mooro. Twice he looked up and stroked the ball into spaces where he knew I'd be. As ever with Mooro, he was right. I was. Without his vision, and calmness under pressure, my hattrick wouldn't exist.

So it's odd to think that I first met him playing cricket.

We were just boys. At that age I was equally keen on two sports. There was no question of divided loyalties. I was pretty good at both and at that age had no preference for one over the other. Football in the winter, cricket in the summer – there was enough space in the calendar to accommodate each enthusiasm.

At a certain point, I was doing well enough for my school team to be selected to play for Essex Schoolboys. I can't pinpoint exactly how old I was but in the photo of the team I still have I'd say I look about 13. There we all are in our smart whites. I'm standing right of centre at the back. I've got a neat side parting and a face that I'm told hasn't changed much over the years. The people who recognise me in the street now would probably be able to tell it's me in the photo.

Also in the photo are two future county cricketers who would go on to play for Essex, and my best man Eddie Presland, who like me would fetch up at West Ham. And guess who that is sitting in the middle at the front, arms folded, smiling widely? Needless to say he was captain, a natural pick as leader even when his voice had only just broken – if it actually had.

There was only one game. We played in Canterbury against Kent Schoolboys. Like me, he was a batter. I can't remember the result, or if I scored some runs or if he did. I didn't know who he was, I may not have even spoken to him. I certainly didn't address him as Mooro. But there we both are, one behind the other, born eight months apart and without a thought of 1966 in our young heads. It's ridiculous to think that there's this matchday snap of Essex Schoolboys, but there is no official photo taken of the team on the day of the World Cup final.

I would know him for the best part of 40 years until his early death at the age of only 51 in 1993. But how well I really knew him is a question I've asked myself ever since.

It's not that he was shy exactly, although he certainly had shy parents. I met his mother Doris – known as Doss – only a couple of times. Apparently she couldn't bear the limelight. Nor could his father Bob. There is a lovely story from Mooro's biography about Bob going to the second World Cup group game. The winger Terry Paine had been called up to help break down the Mexico defence. Mooro arranged tickets for Bob, but his enjoyment of the game was marred by a man in front with a loud voice and a tendency to keep leaping up. Bob overcame his natural timidity enough to ask him to sit down. 'Do you know who I am?' came the reply. 'I'm Terry Paine's father!' Bob was far too introverted to reveal that his own son was Terry Paine's captain.

Some of that must have had an influence on their famous son. He loved a drink, he loved socialising, he enjoyed being a celebrity. Mooro could be funny too. He took great pleasure in cup finals and internationals, when he walked along the line introducing the team to whoever was the guest of honour, in identifying us incorrectly. 'This is George Cohen,' he'd say, presenting Ray Wilson to the visiting dignitary. 'This is Roger Hunt,' he'd say in front of Jimmy Greaves. Mind you, I think he behaved with the Queen at the World Cup.

But he was incredibly private. You never really knew what was going on in his head. This was to his advantage on the field of play, where he had an uncanny ability to keep his cool. And that in turn must have helped him to see the game clearly and therefore consistently to make correct decisions. If you're going to be a great player it helps to have the temperament that enables you to concentrate. I was very much the same in that I never really got involved with altercations on the pitch. I wasn't there to have a row with people, I was there to score goals. But Mooro was next level.

He never seemed to get annoyed. Alan Ball used to say that he didn't give you a bollocking, he just raised his eyebrows and that was enough. If anyone else raised an eyebrow at Bally, who had a ferocious temperament, he'd tell them to eff off! But he would accept a ticking off from Mooro.

I can remember him losing his rag in an international game only once. I think it was against Northern Ireland and the player he had a go at was Derek Dougan, a burly forward who played for Wolves. I can see Mooro now going absolutely nuts at him. I'd love to know what Dougan must have said or done to provoke him, but if I'd asked after the game Mooro would have just smiled and said nothing.

Keeping a lid on it was one expression of his calm character. But he didn't go over the top in the other direction either. It's amazing that I can remember him paying me a compliment because it happened so rarely. Once, in fact. I was at my peak when in a game up at Sunderland I must have played out of my skin. I don't recall what happened on the pitch but I can clearly picture the scene in the dressing room afterwards. They had these big baths at Roker Park but also these smaller slipper baths. I was relaxing in one of those when Mooro sauntered past and sat on the side of the bath. And he swore. That's the other thing that you didn't hear often from him. He liked to mind his Ps and Qs.

'You were absolutely fucking brilliant today,' he said. 'You were absolutely fucking brilliant.'

It was such a surprise. It wasn't just the swearing. It was the praise. He never said anything like that before or after. Not even when I scored six against Sunderland in a home win. Not even after the World Cup final! Mooro was just not that kind of person. If he wasn't prone to explode, he certainly wasn't one to gush.

One thing I am certain of: he was the best footballer I ever played with. I'll go further than that. I've been on the same pitch as some of the greats. Pelé, Eusébio, Beckenbauer. Mooro belonged in their company. There's no doubt in my mind that he was the greatest player in the history of English football. You can forget your Beckhams, your Gascoignes and your Linekers. They're all great players. In fact, only recently they were all voted among the top-ten English players by a poll of German football fans. Also on it, quite rightly, were my teammates Gordon Banks, Bobby Charlton and Jimmy Greaves, as well as Sir Stanley Matthews and Alan Shearer. I confess I'd have been a bit put out if I hadn't made it onto the bottom of the list too. But Mooro stands above us all.

Although he was born in the same year, he was always ahead of me. He joined West Ham earlier, progressed through the system faster than me, and was picked to play for England a good four years before me. He already had 36 caps by the time I made my debut and had already been to a World Cup. So I always looked up to him as a senior player and never lost an opportunity to study the way he worked, the way he trained, the way he conducted himself on and off the pitch. Success and fame would earn him renown as a great role model. But before the rest of the nation cottoned on, he was showing the way to the likes of me.

My first impression of him was how calm and collected he was on the field. Even when we were 17-year-old kids playing for the West Ham youth team that lost to Blackburn Rovers over two legs in the final of the FA Youth Cup, he already had that great ability to read the game. He was almost psychic the way he knew the shape of play as it panned out in front of him. Our manager Ron Greenwood, who was a progressive thinker on the training ground, had an exercise he sometimes liked to make us do when the first team played the reserves. In the middle of a game he'd get us to stop and close our eyes and describe where everyone else was positioned on the pitch at that moment. Mooro was always streets ahead of the rest of us. It was as if he had a sixth sense for spatial awareness.

This was obviously one of his great attributes before he went on to improve in other areas of his game as he progressed from the third team to the reserves and finally the first team.

If his play was immaculate, so was his appearance. His mum Doss went so far as to iron his bootlaces. It was a super-stition of his to put on his shorts just before we walked out. So they'd be hanging on his peg while everyone else was already in their kit. They'd have a nice crease in them, and people often remarked that they came in just as white as when he went out. That sounds like a joke, but he was a very clean tackler. A lot of his work was interceptions rather than 50–50 tackles. Mooro made probably the most famous tackle in the history of the game. As Jairzinho of Brazil was bearing down on England's penalty area in Guadalajara in the 1970 World Cup, Mooro tracked backwards while running sideways, keeping his eye on the ball before ever so deftly, and with an elegant lunge, he planted his right boot on it. If he hadn't been accurate, he'd have got an ankle and Brazil would have had a penalty. Jairzinho went flying while Mooro, having barely lost his footing, calmly rose and dribbled out of the box before stroking the ball upfield. It was less an old-school tackle than a sophisticated intervention. 'What a player this fellow is,' said commentator David Coleman. Yep. The better the opposition, the better he played.

'Look at Mooro, he's absolutely immaculate,' Mike Summerbee once said to me after a game up at Manchester City. He was pointing at Mooro, who was over at the bar. 'He's the only player I know that irons his money.' Mike was a funny guy, and obviously half-remembered that joke when many years later he came to Upton Park as a Man City ambassador. We were in the boardroom together and he recalled playing with Mooro for the same team in a charity match in the off season. 'I see him in the bath after the game,' he said. 'He's the only person who gets out of a bath and he's not wet.'

One of my favourite photographs of us together was taken in the car park at the West Ham training ground. I can date it to 1970, because prior to England's trip to the World Cup in Mexico the players were all loaned a Ford Cortina. Yes I know, a Cortina is hardly comparable with the mega-cars even journeymen players drive nowadays. The photo shows us in the car park as the Cortinas were delivered. I'm sitting on the cream bonnet of one of them wearing a tie and a blazer. Mooro is belted into a brown suede coat, looking ever so suave, like he's stepped out of the brochure. In a sense he had. The coats were one of the side businesses he got into while still playing. Another was flogging memorabilia in a shop near the ground. Then there was the country house club in Epping Forest he co-owned with Sean Connery. (None of these ventures made him a packet – Mooro's business acumen was not on a level with his abilities as a footballer.) I didn't keep my Cortina, though we had an opportunity to buy them quite cheaply. I probably wanted to buy one of those coats off him instead.

Mooro knew how to look good in a photograph. It was as if he'd worked out the most photogenic way of leading the team onto the pitch. He'd stride out with a ball clamped to his left hip by a hand, a wrist or a forearm. It was a pose that projected confidence and composure. One of my favourite images of our World Cup winning team was taken two days after we'd come through the quarter-final against Argentina and the day before the semi-final against Portugal. We were at the training ground in Roehampton and wearing our blue tracksuits. There's no sign of Alf Ramsey but Harold Shepherdson, the physio, stands on the left. It looks as if it was hastily arranged. Nobby Stiles is looking at the floor. So is Bobby Charlton, who is wearing a light-blue pullover. Ray Wilson's eyes are shut. Banksy is biting his lip. For some unrecorded reason, with my arms nervously folded, I'm sitting in the middle of the front row where the captain should be. Our captain, meanwhile, is standing in his preferred place, on the right of the back row where a teacher would be in a school team photo, nonchalantly leaning a forearm on the shoulder of Alan Ball. He looks so cool!

Under the smooth exterior there were faint hints of dissatisfaction. Mainly, Mooro kept his unhappiness firmly bolted down, but I was aware and so were my teammates that he and Ron Greenwood didn't get on at all. They were both brilliant at what they did. They were on the same wavelength on footballing matters. So what was the problem?

Mooro's form for England was never less than fantastic, but his manager felt that wasn't always the case with West Ham.

Ron sometimes had the impression that on a wet Wednesday night somewhere up north, his captain wasn't fully motivated. It's not as if we didn't achieve success on the pitch. In successive seasons, West Ham won the FA Cup (1963–4) and then the European Cup Winners' Cup (1964–5). Towards the end of the following season we were flirting with relegation although, having qualified as winners, we were still in the Cup Winners' Cup and had made it to the semi-final against Borussia Dortmund. Ron decided to take the armband off his captain. He rubbed salt in the wound by giving an interview to the *Daily Mail*. 'Moore has not been really playing for us for eight months … We can't have a man leading the side who doesn't want to play for us.' (We lost to Dortmund, and I didn't score, while across the two legs Lothar Emmerich got four. He would meet three of us Hammers again in the World Cup final three months later, when I'd have better luck against Dortmund's goalkeeper Hans Tilkowski.)

Obviously you notice when you're no longer being led out by your captain. But I would only discover the background to this many years later. Mooro had been out for three months the previous season. We were all told that it was a groin injury. It emerged only after his death that he had testicular cancer and in November 1964 had a testicle removed. For the radiotherapy that came afterwards, he had to have a blue cross marked on his back to help guide the radiographers. I had no idea it was there because – and I don't think I would have twigged at the time – in the dressing room he went to some lengths to make sure no one saw. He was so private that he wouldn't tell anyone, and the news only came out the day before his memorial service at

Westminster Abbey when his first wife Tina gave an interview. Ron visited him in hospital but I wonder if even he knew what the real medical problem was.

Why couldn't they get on? One reason is that Mooro was as much of a closed book to Ron as he was to the rest of us. 'The inner part of his personality,' he once said, 'remains a mystery to me and, I'm sure, to the great majority of those who come in contact with him.' Although they were very different, the irony is that this is one thing they had in common. Neither of them was great at communicating. They were both backward in coming forward. For a manager and a captain, that creates a problem. Ron was a schoolteacher type who didn't dish out praise any more than Mooro did. According to our teammate Harry Redknapp, Mooro resented that. He craved the odd pat on the back, and apparently none ever came. Not that Ron failed to sing his praises in the media. A whole year before the World Cup a journalist was interviewing Ron at Chadwell Heath while the team were out training. The journalist asked about England's chances as hosts. 'We're going to win and that man's the reason why,' said Ron. He pointed at Mooro. What he said next is not just a comment on ability. It also suggested a shrewd understanding of what made his captain tick. 'He can already see in his mind's eye a picture of himself holding up the World Cup and he's calculated what that will mean to him.'

Call it what you want: confidence, sixth sense, positive visualisation. Ron knew that Mooro knew.

Of course, he wouldn't be raising the World Cup if he wasn't selected. Alf had trusted him from the very start. Mooro was only 22, and winning his 12th cap, when in May 1963 he became England's youngest ever captain. He was given the role on a permanent basis the following summer when England went to Rio to play Brazil, Portugal and Argentina for what was known as the Little World Cup. That must have been quite a baptism for him.

But three years on, Alf was definitely puzzled and possibly rattled by Mooro's dip in form for West Ham, and would have been concerned when the club captaincy was taken away from him. When England hosted Yugoslavia in May, just a couple of weeks after West Ham lost to Dortmund, the team selection was notable for two reasons: for the first time, it marked the presence on the team sheet of Martin Peters, but also the absence of Bobby Moore. Then, in a weeklong tour before the World Cup kicked off, England dashed around Europe playing four warm-up friendlies. The first was in Finland on 26 June. It was the last ever cap for the previous captain Jimmy Armfield, Martin scored his first goal for England, and Bobby Moore was still not playing.

I had my own worries on that tour, which also took us to Norway, Denmark and Poland. My form dipped and as a result I was fairly certain that I would not be in the starting line-up for the World Cup. I wouldn't have known what Alf was thinking anyway, because he didn't share his thoughts with the squad. He probably never explained things to Mooro either. But the sight of Jack Charlton playing at the back with Norman Hunter, as they did for Leeds, would surely have concentrated Mooro's mind. For the rest of that tour he was restored to the centre of the defence and, of course, the captaincy.

It was all very well having Mooro back on the pitch. But technically you couldn't actually play for England in the World Cup unless you were attached to a club. The opening game was now days away, and England's captain was not officially a West Ham player.

You can barely imagine him in another shirt. The name of Bobby Moore is inextricably linked with West Ham, but at the time he wanted to leave. However much he liked to keep his cards close to his chest, his unhappiness was loudly rumoured around the club. Did the captaincy and/or the cancer have anything to do with his unhappiness? I can't be certain. I do know that, like all top professionals, Mooro was eager to win trophies and, while he was at it, earn a few more quid. It is surprising to me that he had itchy feet. We'd just won two trophies in consecutive seasons. West Ham had not played at Wembley since it was built in 1923 but under Ron Greenwood suddenly we'd won finals there two years running. In 1966 we also reached the League Cup final, only to lose over two legs to West Brom. But we were never competitive in the league. It must have been with that in mind that Mooro asked if the club would be open to an approach from Spurs. If he was close to anyone in football, he was close to Spurs' star striker Jimmy Greaves, and I'm sure he fancied having him as a clubmate. In those days no player could move unless the club wanted to sell. West Ham didn't want to sell. Meanwhile Mooro was out of contract, and refused to sign a new one. It was a stand-off.

The distraction was a major headache for Alf, who insisted on two prerequisites before he considered anyone for selection. You had to be playing regularly, and you couldn't be unhappy at your club. To be in dispute with your employers was a real black mark against you. So he appealed to Ron Greenwood to sort it out. Ron duly arrived at our team hotel in Hendon, north-west London, and, after a brief negotiation, Mooro signed an extension to his contract that would mean he was a West Ham player until the last day of July. In other words, the day after the final. So it's possible he went through the whole tournament imagining that, in his heart of hearts, he was a Tottenham player.

The disquiet didn't show. He'd been through this terribly disruptive time in the nine months before the World Cup. But Mooro was always relaxed, always up for a laugh. Take the day after England drew 0–0 against Uruguay. Alf arranged for us to visit Pinewood Studios, where Sean Connery was filming *You Only Live Twice*. The James Bond star resisted the temptation to say, 'You never score once.' In fact, he was kind enough to suggest we were unlucky not to put three past Uruguay. The squad was clearly of interest because Yul Brynner, Britt Ekland, George Segal and Norman Wisdom also showed up from their various film sets. 'Is it too late to get in the team?' Wisdom asked. Surprisingly we were allowed a drink or two. We relaxed, signed autographs for young actors and, as he thanked everyone for their hospitality, Alf made his famous gaffe, mispronouncing Connery's first name. Sean came out as Seen. Mooro and Jimmy thought this was hysterical. 'Now I've shorn everything,' said Mooro, quick as a flash.

After one goalless draw, we hadn't shorn anything yet.

The night before the final, Alf chose not to announce the team to the whole group but individually, swearing us all to secrecy as he gave us the good news. The only player he didn't bother to inform was Mooro.

'If Bobby Moore didn't know he was playing without me telling him so,' he said, 'he's not the Bobby Moore I know.'

Our captain took that sharpness of his, that vision, that cool computer brain onto the Wembley grass in 1966, and he played like the god he was.

4

CHELTENHAM

I'm fine with describing Bobby Moore as a deity, because to me he was. I find it baffling and a bit unsettling whenever anyone seems to view me in the same light. In Cheltenham, where I live, there are more than enough people who still apparently recognise the old man that they spot walking around the town, sometimes semi-disguised in a baseball cap. And if they approach, some do seem genuinely to think they're talking to some sort of god. I do struggle with that.

I suppose this is what happens when people put up bronze statues of you. A monumental statue of Mooro stands rightly and proudly outside the new Wembley Stadium. I was there in 2007 when Bobby Charlton unveiled it in front of dignitaries including the prime minister, Tony Blair. Arms folded, a ball under his left foot, gaze off into the middle distance – it's a fitting tribute to a colossus. The plaque says it all, and more:

> Immaculate footballer. Imperial defender. Immortal hero of 1966. First Englishman to raise the World Cup aloft. Favourite son of London's East End. Finest legend of West Ham United. National treasure. Master of Wembley. Lord of the game. Captain extraordinary. Gentleman for all time.

I wouldn't disagree with any of that.

The sculptor was Philip Jackson, who has put his name to many a well-known public statue in central London: he's also done bronzes of the Queen and Gandhi and the men of Bomber Command. This wasn't his first one of Mooro. Another one has stood outside West Ham's old ground at Upton Park since 2003. The difference is I'm in that one too. It depicts Ray Wilson and me holding our captain on our shoulders as he brandishes the Jules Rimet trophy, while I'm arm in arm with Martin Peters standing by my side. In 2021, several years after the club moved to the London Stadium, a new statue was created, this one showing Martin and me bearing the weight of Mooro as he holds aloft the European Cup Winners' Cup we won in 1965. The details are absolutely bang on: as was the case back in the day, Martin's the only one of us wearing shinpads.

Some might think that two statues with me in them is enough to be going on with. Actually there are three. The third is less well known. It's an all-action statue of the three World Cup winners who hail from the borough of Tameside in Greater Manchester – me, my 1966 squad mate Jimmy Armfield, and Simone Perrotta, who won playing for Italy in 2006. It was placed on a plinth in the centre of a roundabout by a local sports centre in 2010. Perhaps it could have been better publicised: Perrotta didn't find out about it for another seven years!

Most people who know who I am probably have no idea that I was born where I was. It makes me the odd one out among my teammates. We were Englishmen first and foremost, a united side with no cliques, brought together because of what we had in common: 11 hard-nosed professionals who Alf Ramsey knew he could trust. But it's also true that the England team that won the World Cup was a blend. A blend of world-class and solid supporting players. A blend of experience and youth – from Ray Wilson, our oldest player at 31, to Alan Ball, our youngest at 21. I find it interesting that those born before the war would go on to do National Service, while the rest of us escaped it. Jack Charlton did two years in the Household Cavalry in Germany, where he captained the Horse Guards. His brother Bobby spent his time with the Royal Army Ordnance Corps in Shrewsbury, turning out for Man U on Saturdays. Roger Hunt joined Liverpool only after leaving the army at 21. Ray did his time in the Middle East and hated it so much he had 'Egypt never again' tattooed on his forearm. It was life-changing for Gordon Banks, who served with the Royal Signals in Germany, where he met his future wife Ursula.

But the biggest and clearest dividing line was between north and south. The Charltons came from Northumberland, Nobby, Roger and Bally from Lancashire, Banksy and Ray from Yorkshire. Mooro, Martin and George Cohen were all Londoners.

I had a foot in both camps. I was born on 8 December 1941 in Ashton-under-Lyne on the outskirts of Manchester. That makes me a northerner by birth. But when I was six my father got a job in Essex as a toolmaker and we moved down to Chelmsford. So I became a southerner.

Life and work has taken me all over the place since then. In 1972, after ten years in the first team at West Ham, the club decided to let me go. Wondering where to head next, I joined Banksy at Stoke City. When we first arrived we were kindly lent a house by George Eastham, my fellow World Cup squad member who had been at the club since 1966. We lived up there for several years. Like many an ex-footballer, I even bought a pub in the area and we kept it for five years. At the same time, I got into management, taking up a job at non-league Telford United. The family came back south again in 1979 when I had an offer to be coach, then manager, at Chelsea. We based ourselves in Cobham in Surrey. Then we spent two years in Kuwait where I had a coaching job, and moved back to Surrey when I decided to give up working in football and look for something with a bit more job security.

Entering the insurance industry was, again, a common choice for former players back in those days. I stuck at it until my retirement. The date I quit was actually delayed by four years. I decided to leave business in 1998, by which time I was quite heavily involved in public speaking and England's campaign to bring the World Cup back home as hosts of the 2006 tournament. But when I chucked my company car keys on the desk of my boss, he chucked them straight back at me, so I stayed on part-time for two days a week until 2002. They barely used me in those years so I was essentially paid to twiddle my thumbs. Judith used to tease me about it. 'I'm sure you drive to the office, drive round the building, and then come home again.'

By then, I was a grandfather, and very much involved in the lives of the two children of our oldest daughter Claire. Perhaps we might have stayed in Surrey for the rest of our lives. But at a certain point Claire's marriage broke down and she expressed a desire to move away. But where?

Only a year earlier I had spoken to a group of leavers at a school in Cheltenham called Dean Close. I was invited along thanks to my good friend Terry Hopley, who had been editor of a local east London paper when I was at West Ham and came round every Sunday to interview me for my weekly column. He had no fewer than seven grandchildren at the school. While there I had a nose round and was impressed. So Claire looked into getting a place for her daughter Amy. The move was complicated by the fact that her son Jack needed to stay on at his school as moving at his particular age would be disruptive. So we reached a compromise. Judith and I rented a house in Cheltenham and Amy lived with us for that school year. You could almost say we became her adoptive parents. Then we saw an apartment building that we liked in a lovely part of Cheltenham and we have lived there ever since.

Gradually, a family that had begun in Essex and had been relocated to Stoke and then three consecutive homes in Surrey, started moving piece by piece to Gloucestershire. After a year, Claire followed with Jack. Our middle daughter Joanne came west too. Then one day I had a phone call from our youngest daughter Charlotte, who was living and working back in the south of England. 'Dad, I'm getting married,' she said, 'and we're coming to live near you.'

We're like iron filings, the Hurst family. Charlotte went on to have three children. As I started working on this book, the oldest, George, was due to leave school, Grace turned 15 and Rose seven. I'm very close to them all. To have the family nearby is very good for us and there's no doubt it's good for them, and not just because some get chauffeured home from school by their grandpa every day. Jack runs a gym here. Only Amy has moved back towards her roots, working for her father's business.

Every one of us is very close in a way that wasn't the case in the family I grew up in. I barely saw my mother's parents, who lived in Gloucestershire. More damagingly, my own parents started to withdraw from our lives around about the time England won the World Cup. We never worked out why this was, but it felt as if they started to treat me more as a celebrity than as their son, and behaved like nervous fans rather than parents. They seemed to think that Judith and I had passed through some sort of looking glass into the world of limos and champagne. This wasn't the case at all, but the unfortunate result was that they were not involved in the lives of the only grandchildren they would ever have. When my parents divorced the emotional distance widened even further. My father remarried and his wife would have nothing to do with his family at all. Neither of my parents came to Claire's wedding in 1987.

I can't say if it has been a conscious decision, or just an instinctive reaction, but Judith and I have made sure that there are no such barriers in our family. We're all in one another's pockets all the time, and everyone gets on. Our youngest granddaughters treat our oldest granddaughter like an extra aunt. It's standard practice for three generations of Hursts to go on three-week summer holidays together, often to Barbados. Judith and I do our own thing in the daytime and then we all meet up in the evening to eat and laugh and take the mickey out of one another.

Cheltenham may seem an unlikely place for me to make my home. It's got a racing festival, a literary festival and a jazz festival but, with the greatest respect to the local club, it's not exactly a footballing hotbed. It's a quiet, pleasant town, and that suits me well.

While I do get recognised, of course there are some people who don't give a shit who I am or genuinely have no idea. So it balances out. I lead a normal life. My wife makes sure of that. To reduce the likelihood of my being identified when we go to cafés and restaurants, Judith always sits me in the chair facing the wall while she's the one who looks out. So I rarely know if anyone's looking at me but Judith's radar will soon work out if I've been spotted and become the subject of quiet nods and whispers on other tables. Unlike the wives of some footballers, she has gone to great lengths to make damn sure that no one knows what she looks like. She values her anonymity. Whenever someone does happen to ask if she's the wife of Geoff Hurst – or, worse still, addresses her as Lady Hurst – she has perfected a silent stare that could reverse global warming! Mind you, she won't let me get away with frostiness. When people do come up and want to shake my hand, she tells me that my face some-times betrays my discomfort, and that I could make an effort to look a bit more cheerful. I guess that comes with a lifetime of being hailed for the events of a single afternoon nearly six decades ago.

There's no doubt that winning the World Cup has shaped my life. I've been doing an occasional theatre tour since 2017, and in 2024 I set out on what my agent Terry Baker, who is also a very good friend, decided to call a farewell tour. It could turn out to be a long goodbye. I know I can't keep going forever, but every time I turn my back I notice that Terry's bunged on another set of dates. Judith says I've had more farewells than Frank Sinatra. The reality is that, like other guest appearances I'm invited to make, they get me out of the house and they keep me busy. I like to be active and prefer having things in the diary. There's a theory I buy into that if you slow down too much you might seize up altogether.

However long the shows last, they've been tremendously rewarding to do. In the first half I share my memories of 1966, although the subject might stray towards the present. For example, after Kylian Mbappé scored two goals for France against Argentina in the World Cup final in Qatar in 2022, I had a hunch that in a minute he was going to become the second man to score a hattrick in the final and I needed to work out what to say about it. I released a congratulatory tweet that night as soon as my premonition came to pass. I've had a very good run, but in my theatre show I gently argue that his hattrick includes two penalties and he finished on the losing side. Always gets a big clap, that.

One reliable way of keeping people entertained is to quote the quick wit of Jimmy Greaves. A wicked quip of his I enjoy sharing is from the time three of us were invited to attend an event at Wembley in 2014. Jimmy, Banksy and I were there as guests of FIFA, who with the World Cup finals about to be played in Brazil were touring the trophy around all the partici-pating nations. But before the official event we were preparing to do a Q&A at a breakfast meeting with a box holder at the stadium. Someone from the FA primed us with some serious questions. One of them was, 'What is the most important piece of half-time information you received from Alf Ramsey during your time as England player?' I was first up and said that, although I didn't recall anything from half time, I did remember his talk between full time and extra time in the final, culminating in his famous exit line: 'You've beat them once, now go and beat them again.' (Or words to that effect: recollections of his precise wording vary.) Banksy was asked the same question, and I've no idea what he said. We get to Jimmy. All laid back and laconic, he says, 'Well, I was playing a few years before Alf took over. His first game at Wembley, not sure who against, we were playing very poorly. At half time Alf comes in, looked at everybody in the room, then focused on me and said, "Jimmy, put your fag out."'

After the interval comes the Q&A, when I have to be on my toes because people might ask anything. The audience will also include people eager to share. A lot of them are Hammers. Someone brought along a programme from my first game for West Ham, the month I turned 17 in 1958. One night a man told me his mother went to school in Barking with Mooro and remembered that even then he was immaculate. Another man told me he'd changed the name of his house to Hurstmoore, and showed me a photo to prove it.

Even though Judith says I can look a little bit grumpy sometimes, I happily sign anything people ask me to. The most unusual rarity I've signed came to me via the bloke who cleans our windows. It was an unused set of World Cup final tickets from 1966. They were a sort of family heirloom, presented to a local builder who often took part payment in anything his customers offered him: Barbour jackets, wellington boots or, on one occasion, tickets to Wembley Stadium on 30 July 1966. On the day of the final the family happened to be on holiday in Torquay. So two seats on the greatest day in English football history went unoccupied.

In my theatre show, I always make a point of giving a stock answer to one question before anyone has the chance to ask it: 'Did the ball cross the line?' As I always say, I'm the wrong person to ask as I was flat on my back and various West Germans were in the way so I had the worst view in the stadium, etc. Roger Hunt was convinced it was a goal and turned away to celebrate and so on and so on. I've had the answer off pat for decades now. If only I had a quid for every time I've been asked …

In a sense the debate about that goal has been the most lasting memento of the final. But I keep a store of other souvenirs in our spare bedroom. Photos, programmes, documents, commemorative books. Their value is purely personal. Almost all the stuff with any value was sold at auction in 2000 – apart, that is, from the things that were half-inched in a burglary when we were living in Surrey. The sale came about after a gentle chat with my three daughters. We're really not a celebrity family and I was wondering if there was any stuff they would be interested in having. I was thinking about my medals but Claire said, 'Dad, in the living room is a lovely settee, I'd like that.' She wasn't joking. I decided to cash it all in. This spared my family the hassle of dealing with it after I'm gone. Also it seemed shrewd to put it up for auction while there were still enough collectors around who might want to buy it.

Christie's South Kensington produced a handsome, glossy catalogue containing 129 lots. They included all sorts of memorabilia – medals and trophies, shirts and tracksuits, balls and caps, even a bronze plaster bust of me. The oldest item – Lot 1 – was a bronze plaque presented to me in 1959 as a runner-up in the FA Youth Cup when West Ham lost to Blackburn. The most valuable included my two winner's medals in the FA Cup and the Cup Winners' Cup, the England cap I won for playing three games in the 1966 World Cup, my silver man-of-the-match trophy voted by the readers of the *News of the World*, and of course my shirt. Proceeds from 18 of the lots went to the Brain and Spine Foundation and the Bobby Moore Fund for Cancer Research.

Preparing for the sale introduced me to the very specific way of doing things that they have at auction houses. A mantel clock given to me by the West Ham Supporters Club 'to honour his part in helping England win the World Cup' was listed as having 'one foot lacking'. I was unable to account for the damage. They needed to list every lot as precisely as possible. Take Lot 8. I'd have described it as quite an attractive medal from a European Championship where England should have done better. Christie's went into more detail.

> A bronze European Nations Cup Third Place Winner's medal, the obverse cast with the map of Europe and a football, the reverse inscribed UEFA, Championnat D'Europe, 1968, III e Rang, with ribbon, in original fitted case. In the match played on 8th June 1968 in Rome, England defeated the USSR 2–0 to win the 3rd and 4th place play-off. Bobby Charlton opened the scoring in the 39th minute and Geoff Hurst doubled England's tally in the 63rd. Estimate £800–£1,200.

Quite a mouthful, eh?

I couldn't always supply the information Christie's were after. Although I wasn't a great one for exchanging shirts at the end of a game, I did have a few in my possession. The one from the DDR (as in Deutsche Demokratische Republik/ German Democratic Republic, as East Germany was known) was a bit of a collectors' item, being from a country that by 2000 no longer existed. I knew exactly who had given it to me in 1970: a centre back called Klaus Sammer. But a problem arose with Scotland. I played Scotland six times and had three shirts to show for it. This was before YouTube became a handy video library of old games, which would have enabled forensic examination of Scotland's varying badge designs. So it was harder to pin down which Scot I'd swapped my shirt with. Hence the confusion in the listing: 'The above shirt was gained as a swop [sic] with either Jim Baxter, 2/4/66, 15/4/67, John Greig, 10/5/69 or Bobby Moncur, 25/4/70, 22/5/71. Estimate £300–£500.'

It would probably have had a great deal more value if we'd been able to pin it down to 15/4/67. That was the infamous day when Scotland came to Wembley and beat England 3–2. After their win Scotland were soon crowning themselves the real world champions, and bragged that because Jimmy Greaves was playing, the England team they'd beaten was even stronger than the one that defeated West Germany nine months earlier.

Unfortunately there was no way of knowing which shirt in my collection was exchanged on that day. It might have been with Jim Baxter because his shirt had a six on it. It's just as likely to have been Baxter's shirt from the year before, when we won 4–3 at Hampden Park and I opened the scoring in my second ever game for England. That shirt, associated with an England away win, would have a lot less appeal to a Scottish collector.

The newspapers reporting on the sale often went for a variation on Kenneth Wolstenholme's famous line of commentary. My favourite was in the *Middlesbrough Evening Gazette*: 'And folk say modern kits are too dear.' The whole collection realised £274,410.

I didn't include the most valuable item of all: my World Cup winner's medal. George Cohen had sold his two years earlier to help fund his retirement, and it was bought by his old club Fulham. I wanted to keep mine separate and make sure that, like George's, it ended up in the hands of the right owner. My reason for selling was practical. It was the same for all my teammates who cast sentiment aside to sell their winner's medal. I had more than one child, and while it remained in my possession the medal had a value that could not be evenly distributed. My old club, which had already bought Mooro's medal, made overtures, and the year after the Christie's auction I arranged for a sale agreement to be drawn up between West Ham United Football Club and my three daughters. The medal ended up in the club museum alongside those of Mooro and Martin Peters, who sold his in the same year.

The sale of my memorabilia didn't stop there. At Christie's my shirt ('No 10, with crew-neck collar and embroidered cloth badge') sold for £91,750, which was then a world record for a football shirt. The anonymous Spurs fan who bought it was at the final in 1966. In 2008 he sold it on for an undisclosed sum to a group of international investors. When they in turn tried to auction it at Sotheby's on the 50th anniversary of the World Cup win in 2016, it didn't reach its reserve price of £300,000.

I'm not sure what to make of this. I didn't stand to gain from the sale, but had something to lose from its non-sale. I suppose it's healthy to be brought down a peg or two. It happens all the time. Years ago, I was in London for a promotional function and the following morning I was flying out of Heathrow to do something in Europe. I get in the back of a black cab. I'm reading a big broadsheet paper but when I look up I see the cabbie's eyes staring at me in the rear-view mirror. I go back to my paper but have this feeling I can't shake that he's still staring at me. I look up and, sure enough, he is. On this goes, all the way to the airport. It's only in the tunnel at Heathrow that he breaks the silence.

'Oi, mate,' he says. 'Give us a clue.'

'My name's Sir Geoff Hurst,' I say. 'I played for West Ham and England, and scored a hattrick in the World Cup final.'

'Don't be a prat,' he says. 'Which terminal do you want?'

And it's still happening. Not long ago in Cheltenham I was just coming out of John Lewis when a man tapped me on the shoulder. 'Excuse me,' he said. 'Please can I have your autograph?' He didn't have anything for me to write on other than his paper shopping bag so that's where I put my signature. Then I carried on and suddenly there was another tap on the shoulder. This time it was a woman.

'I saw you signing that autograph,' she said. 'I know who you are. You're Glenn Hoddle.'

5

THE GHOST

Hindsight being what it is, it's sometimes hard to see back beyond the World Cup in 1966 and picture it as an event that was yet to happen. Because of what took place on the day itself, lives were changed and names were made, and some of us even found ourselves cast in bronze. But when it was all still in the future, we didn't have the benefit of hindsight. Nor foresight, come to that. I can honestly say that Martin Peters and I did not picture ourselves as World Cup winners. Not for one second. We hadn't the foggiest idea that we might end up in the England squad, let alone the team, let alone playing key roles in the final. We even planned a summer holiday in Cornwall with some teammates and our families, and actually managed to fit it in. In the beginning, we were not in the picture. That's the thing no one now remembers.

Martin was to be known as the Ghost. The nickname came about because he had an unusual skill in a footballer: he could slip into dangerous areas unnoticed. He specialised in appearing unawares in the box at the last minute and scoring. Martin wouldn't be there, and then suddenly he would.

His arrival in the England team lived up to that reputation for stealth. Two months before the World Cup he wasn't in the team, or even the squad. The door is closing, the press are all looking the other way and Martin glides into an advanced position and there he is, spiriting into view at the eleventh hour.

No one was more surprised than Martin to find himself playing in the World Cup final, but maybe he shouldn't have been. After all, he played for England Schoolboys against West Germany at Wembley in front of a crowd of nearly 100,000 spectators. He was only 15. Imagine. The largest crowd I played in front of at an equivalent age was for Essex Schoolboys, when next to nobody was watching. This was in 1959. One of the German players, who Martin would meet again on the same pitch seven years later (and again in Mexico four years on from that), was Wolfgang Overath.

Soon Martin progressed to the England Youth team, which was coached by Billy Wright, then the most capped player in England's history. Many of the young players who were selected alongside Martin became successful professionals. Ron Harris – later known as Chopper – went on to acquire a fearsome reputation as an uncompromising tackler at Chelsea. George Armstrong won the league and FA Cup double with Arsenal in 1971. Jim Montgomery had that incredible display in Sunderland's goal in the 1973 FA Cup final, keeping out everything Leeds could throw at him. Terry Venables would manage Spurs, Barcelona and England. But only Martin, who was eventually made England Youth captain, properly made it as an international.

Then he got into the Under 23 squad. This was at the suggestion of Ron Greenwood. The then manager Walter Winterbottom was asking after Bobby Moore. 'Why don't you have a look at Martin Peters?' Ron replied. He won six caps at that level under Winterbottom – back then the England manager oversaw both squads. As soon as Alf Ramsey succeeded him, Martin was no longer picked. Why this should be is a mystery. Perhaps Alf overlooked him on account of something that was more or less unique to Martin. No one knew what his best position was. Martin didn't, and Ron didn't. I suppose Alf couldn't be expected to either.

Martin got into the West Ham first team in dramatic circumstances. We'd just lost and Ron dropped half the team, including me. Martin took my place and Mooro was made captain for the first time.

This was in Easter 1962, back in the era when clubs would play three fixtures in four days over the holiday. In the first game, at home to Cardiff City, we won 4–1. The very next day we welcomed Arsenal and he started again at right half. Then our keeper Lawrie Leslie broke his finger and, there being no substitutes back then, he was shuffled out to the wing and replaced in goal. Martin ended up at left back. Somehow West Ham retrieved a two-goal deficit and drew 3–3. Martin kept a press cutting in his scrapbook: 'Geoff Hurst may have the hardest job winning back his place, for 18-year-old Peters, at wing-half, showed all the promise and poise expected of an England Youth team skipper.' West Ham keepers must have been living under a curse that Easter, because when we went to Cardiff the replacement goalie dislocated a collarbone, and who should pull on the green jersey and deputise between the sticks but Martin? 'Young Peters is a real player,' Ron told the press, 'one of the most versatile I've come across.' Too right! In his first three games in the first team he'd already played in three positions.

So it went on. The next season he began at left back but then replaced me again at right half. Including that stint in goal, he eventually wore every shirt for West Ham from 1 to 11. Mainly he shuttled between defence and midfield. He was the footballing equivalent of a Swiss Army knife. Alf ignored this bit-part player for two whole years.

Another vanishing act Martin had no control over came over Christmas 1963 when West Ham lost 8–2 at home to Blackburn Rovers. Ron was incensed. But when a few days later we played them again at Ewood Park, the only player he dropped was Martin. We played much better and for the rest of the season he only ever returned to the first team as an occasional spare part. It was almost as if Ron had a superstition that to recall him would reverse our luck. Unfortunately for Martin we went on a run all the way to the Cup final, which we won. So two years before Jimmy Greaves stood on the edge of the pitch and watched England do a lap of honour without him, Martin experienced exactly that feeling. On this occasion he was the wrong sort of ghost, haunting the touchline in a suit. He was honest enough to admit that he never quite got over the disappointment.

Alf didn't make many mistakes but he made one about Martin. For some reason, he decided that Martin couldn't head a ball. I have no idea how he came to this absurd conclusion. No one at West Ham was better at it, and I include myself in that. As a tall centre forward I practised heading incessantly, and I got good at it. But I wasn't as good as Martin. He could do everything: head, pass, cross, attack, defend, tackle.

It wasn't until 1968 that Alf issued his celebrated appraisal of Martin's abilities. 'Peters is ten years ahead of his time,' he said. Martin was flattered but at the same time didn't quite know what to make of this judgement. While it sounded like a compliment, he worried it implied that he was neither one thing nor the other. Only when the Dutch brand of total football emerged in the early 1970s did he start to understand it. Suddenly players in orange shirts were doing what Martin had been doing for the best part of a decade. They were making themselves comfortable in any position. Perhaps this is what Ron meant too. 'He's not a typical English player,' he said, 'but he's the answer to a manager's prayer.'

Martin had been playing first-team football for four years but was still only 22 and so eligible for the Under 23 team when Alf at last overcame his blind spot. Martin's eventual call-up to the squad was partly down to Ron, who continued to force his utility player down Alf's throat. 'You've got to pick this guy,' he would say. 'He's brilliant.'

So Martin was picked to play for the Under 23s against Turkey on 20 April 1966. It can't have been lost on him that the game was at Ewood Park, where Ron had left him out two years earlier. On 4 May he won his first England cap against Yugoslavia. From there he made it into the provisional 40-strong pool. He survived the first cull and joined the squad of 27 players who went to train at Lilleshall, the FA's training centre. Five players were sent home when the final squad of 22 was announced, and Martin was still there. It's typical of him that when he heard, he immediately felt bad for Gordon Milne, the much more experienced player he thought he'd displaced.

He was given the squad number of 16. This implied to him – if to no one else – that he was not considered a first-choice pick. It wasn't a watertight theory, because I was given the number 10 and I didn't play in the first three games. Meanwhile Roger Hunt was 21, and he played in all six. But then, in the second group game against Mexico, Martin was in the team. Suddenly, and at the very last moment, the Ghost had ghosted into position.

No one benefitted from Martin's arrival in the squad more than me. In training at West Ham we had this game where you'd chip a ball from the edge of the box and try to hit the crossbar. The player who was better than anybody else was Martin. I was on the end of Martin's laser-guided crosses for seven years at West Ham. A telepathy between us developed over hours and hours of practice at Chadwell Heath, often done after everyone else had finished for the day. In the quarter-final against Argentina he fired an inch-perfect cross to the near post where he knew I'd be to meet it. It's now amazing to me that the cross came from his left foot. My recollection of Martin is of a predominantly one-footed player, but when I go back and watch the old videos on YouTube my memory turns out to be playing tricks on me. So he was even better than I remember!

What of Martin the man? Probably no footballer knew him better than I did, but he was no open book. Like Mooro, he could be quite hard to read, though for less complicated reasons. Where Mooro had the mysterious air of someone who didn't want to be known, Martin just very quietly kept himself to himself. He was easy-going and unassuming. In a word, an introvert. He wasn't an obviously passionate man, which may explain why, although he was devoted to playing football from a young age, he wasn't that interested in watching it. He grew up in Dagenham, so you'd expect him to be a born-and-bred Hammer, but no. Nor did he grow up idolising a favourite player.

On the pitch and off, Martin rarely put his feelings on display. Because he didn't speak much, you wouldn't always know what he was thinking. On the bus to games, and especially as the newest member of the team, he was much the most silent. He never went in for the raucous banter and relentless chatter that seemed to fuel Alan Ball and Jack Charlton, or the more vocal players in the West Ham squad. Martin put a value on discipline and self-control. He'd never get involved in tussles on the pitch, although he could certainly look after himself. This isn't to suggest that his placid demeanour made him somehow characterless. Quite the reverse. He was such an interesting person, maybe because he had this sphinx-like quality that always kept you guessing. Also he had a dry sense of humour and a twinkle in his eye, which came out in the way he always addressed Bobby Moore. Everyone else called our captain Mooro. Martin opted for Robert. It sounded formal, but it was obviously affectionate, and tongue in cheek.

At the same time he was quite prepared to open himself to ridicule. Once when West Ham were playing in a tournament in New York, we travelled on a very tight budget. We were given $5 a day to cover all meals. Martin was saving up to get married that summer and decided he could make the per diem go that little bit further by reusing his teabag. I can still see it now. He'd lower the bag on a string into the cup, keep it in the water for about half as long as normal, lift it out and carefully lay it aside to use it again a second time. Donald Pleasence did something very similar with tea leaves in *The Great Escape*, released in 1963, not long before the tournament. Maybe that's where he got the idea. Only Martin wasn't a prisoner of war and, as we never ceased to tease him, with each weak cuppa he was probably saving point one millionth of a dollar.

As the two young Hammers in the England squad we came to rely on each other. I'd got picked a few months earlier than him. I can't remember who he roomed with when he first joined the squad, but it wouldn't have been me. Alf had a theory that team bonding was best built up by avoiding the formation of cliques. So clubmates were often kept apart. There was no parting Bobby Moore from Jimmy Greaves, or Bobby Charlton from Ray Wilson. The keepers Ron Springett and Peter Bonetti were put together. Nobby Stiles and Alan Ball were natural room-mates. But for whatever reason, by the time we got to Hendon Hall Hotel for the finals, Martin and I were sharing a room. Because we'd already been teammates for years, it was natural for us to confide in each other. In the privacy of our hotel room we'd filled the spare hours talking about team selection, never more intensely than in the three days before the final. Players might not do it nowadays, but we weren't above scouring the papers to see what the football reporters were saying.

Not long after marrying towards the end of 1964, Martin and his wife Kathy moved to Hornchurch. Their new neigh-bours were none other than the Hursts. Our wives were already good pals – Kathy had been Judith's bridesmaid at our wedding. They were so familiar with each other that they wouldn't visit via the front door, instead clambering onto the coalbunker, clearing the fence and coming in via the kitchen door at the back. On Saturday evenings after an away match, Judith always joked that she'd see Martin walking past her window as he returned home, usually hours before I made it back. I was out enjoying a drink, but my neighbour wasn't one for burning the midnight oil out on the town.

That level-headed character was evident on the pitch. He was a fantastic player, but without the swagger of one. His natural modesty worked to his advantage, because opponents could never quite assess the threat he presented or be alert to his subtlety of movement. To this day, it's my firm belief that he has been underrated and thus has never been given the credit he deserves. The injustice of it genuinely irritates me. I'm not sure why it's happened, but I can make a guess. After the World Cup it wasn't lost on anyone, least of all the club and its fans, that the final had prominently featured three players from West Ham. Much was made of us. For the first game of the 1966–7 season, only three weeks after the final, we trotted out onto the pitch at Upton Park ahead of our teammates and took the applause. (We did the same again a week later with Gordon Banks when playing Leicester City at Filbert Street.) There was immense pride in the East End at the contribution made by the club's trio. But there was a hierarchy. Mooro was lofted onto a pedestal for evermore as the captain and figurehead. I got put there as well because of the hattrick. It's my feeling that Martin, maybe because he didn't like calling attention to himself, has been slightly overlooked by posterity. It's as if he was the George Harrison of the three of us. In his autobiography he called himself the third man. While he always insisted that it never bothered him, it did cause him to be nudged out of the limelight that Mooro and I couldn't avoid even if we wanted to. Martin didn't want it. He wanted to disappear back into normal life, and if that meant turning down commercial opportunities that came with fame, so be it.

It took Martin a long time to tear himself away from Upton Park, but in the spring of 1970 he fulfilled an ambition that proved beyond the powers of Bobby Moore: he went to Tottenham. Hammers fans have long since got used to seeing their home-grown stars leave for bigger clubs – think of Tony Cottee, Rio Ferdinand, Julian Dicks, Frank Lampard, Joe Cole, Jermain Defoe, Michael Carrick and, most recently, Declan Rice. Martin was the first of them. My hunch is that his disappointment at missing the Cup final in 1964 smouldered for years. He was also frustrated by our inability to sustain a decent campaign in the First Division. Eventually he couldn't wait to try winning honours elsewhere. But the thing that really wound him up was Ron Greenwood's suggestion that he played better for England than he did for West Ham. Martin had great professional pride and that wounded him.

He would go on to play 67 games for England, eventually being made captain by Alf. Of his 20 goals, none was as important as the ultimate ghost goal he scored in the World Cup final. The score was 1–1. There were 78 minutes on the clock and there hadn't been a goal for nearly an hour. Then Bally sent in a corner from the right, which glanced a German head on the penalty spot. The ball drifted on to me loitering outside the box to the left of the D. After a couple of shimmies I lined up a shot which I slightly mishit. It struck a defender's shin and looped upwards. While the Germans were guilty of ball-watching, with typical discretion Martin quietly held the space he'd been instructed to occupy for corners, while Jack Charlton bustled round the outside of him. Jack always joked he was glad the ball didn't land at his feet because he'd definitely have volleyed it over the bar. In fact, he was much more skilful than his reputation suggests. Still, perhaps it's just as well that when the ball came down at the edge of the six-yard box the player on the end of it, ready to shoelace it firmly between the keeper and the German on the post, was Martin. He was totally unmarked. No one, seemingly, had spotted him. And he was never going to miss.

Of course, everything would have been different if the Germans hadn't equalised with the last meaningful kick of the 90 minutes. (The very last kick before the whistle was taken by me in the centre circle at the restart.) In that case, Martin would have been known as the man who scored the winner. As the striker who got the first goal, my name would be much less prominent in the history books. He used to get a big laugh out of this on the after-dinner speaking circuit. If he hadn't scored, he'd joke, West Germany would have won 2–1.

His bitter regret on that day was that his parents weren't there to see him score. All the players were offered complimentary tickets to the final. Martin, who in the early years of his marriage remained conscious about money, took the opportunity to sell two of his to the notorious tout 'Fat' Stan Flashman. It was a bit naive of him, and meant that his parents had to watch the game on TV. Later, whenever his mother was asked what it was like to see her son win the World Cup, she would say, 'I don't know, we weren't invited.' Martin judged himself harshly for that.

Meanwhile, out on the pitch, our names were conjoined forever that day. Two friends and neighbours, both winning our eighth caps, both names on the scoreboard: experience could not have brought us any closer together. And yet that night Martin was still very much Martin. After the big and frankly boring gala dinner at the Royal Garden Hotel in Kensington, the rest of us were in the mood to celebrate and went out on the tiles. This had been planned even in the event of England losing. We'd barely seen our other halves in weeks. So Judith and I asked Martin and Kathy if they'd like to join us at Danny La Rue's club. Nobby Stiles and his wife Kay, Bally and his girl-friend Lesley, and John Connelly and his wife Sandra all said yes. Martin had been away from Kathy and their baby daughter for two months. He'd missed his wife turning 21 on the day of the France game. On the eve of the final, she'd even had to move house, all on her own because obviously her husband was otherwise engaged. So at the last minute, Martin decided he didn't want to join us.

Thus, after the sun went down on the biggest day of his life, and as the rest of us painted the town red, the Ghost disappeared into the night.

6

THE MEDIEVAL DAYS

The event we're talking about in this book happened when I was 24. By the time anyone reads this, I'll be turning 83. In the intervening decades there have been massive changes in every area of all our lives. I hardly need to list them here. But those changes have been reflected on the football pitch too. Every single aspect of the game has transformed out of all recognition. The only thing that's stayed the same is the goalposts.

Let's begin at the beginning: young talent. At the risk of sounding like a grumpy old man, I don't agree with eight- and nine-year-olds being associated with professional football clubs. How can you possibly tell what a child of that age is going to do? I'm glad to learn that some countries are now raising the lower age limit because it puts a lot of pressure on kids who are selected that early. Alfred Galustian, a very good friend of mine who has worked as an instructor of coaches with many top clubs including Bayern, Real Madrid, Manchester United and City, Roma and Benfica, likes to ask this question about another of his clubs. How many kids that joined Juventus at eight years of age have made the first team over a period of 20 years? The answer is one. One!

My own staggered entry into football is just one of the things that would never happen now. The London scouts didn't come to Chelmsford, but as I wasn't too bad at football at school a friend of my father wrote to West Ham and Arsenal requesting a trial. West Ham were the ones who replied. So I started there in my mid-teens after leaving school. But – and this is the thing that would now be impossible – I remained a keen cricketer. The earliest item in my collection of scrapbooks goes all the way back to 1957 when the *Essex Weekly* reported that I showed 'exceptional promise both as a cricketer and a footballer'. The previous Saturday, they added, I'd made my debut for the Chelmsford first team against South Essex Waterworks, and scored 56 not out. Geoffrey, they said, 'will be returning to Upton Park in the coming season'. I was soon spotted by the county and started going to coaching on Tuesdays and Thursdays, then made it into the lower-level teams just as I was working my way up at West Ham. It seems crazy to think that back then it was perfectly possible to keep both balls in the air. Quite a few managed it in the era before mine – Denis and Leslie Compton and Willie Watson particularly stick in my memory. A few even managed it after me, but only by heavily prioritising cricket and dabbling in football on the side.

For a while, it worked for me. Come the end of the football season I became an Essex player for the months of summer, and was so committed to it that I would miss all the pre-season football training in July. How good a batsman was I? It's hard to know whether I'd have made it. The peak of my cricketing career was brief. Blink and you'd have missed it. In my only first-class game, I was chosen to represent Essex in the County Championship. I was a last-minute selection, put in prematurely because one or two players weren't available. We played

Lancashire in Liverpool and, despite being a batsman, I went in at number 10. There were no helmets back then, and they must have thought I wasn't really ready to be facing the likes of Colin Hilton and Ken Higgs. I didn't trouble the scorers, but in the first innings I can at least claim they didn't get me out. (They did in the second.) In the Essex side was the great England spin bowler Jim Laker, who not many years earlier had taken 19 out of 20 Australian wickets in a Test match at Old Trafford. In Lancashire's second innings I took a catch off Laker's bowling. So I can say that, thanks to one ball, the name of a future World Cup winner is linked with the best spinner England had ever produced. One for the sports anoraks, perhaps. We won. I'm not going to claim I remember much more about Laker, or Lancashire, or the match.

That was over three days between May and June 1962. I've still got the scorecard. I carried on playing for the rest of the summer and got back to Chadwell Heath in mid-September, as usual lacking the two months of conditioning that the rest of my teammates had built up since July. One Saturday, I played a reserve game when still overweight from four months in cricket whites. Back at the training ground on the Monday morning, Ron Greenwood came over. I thought I was going to get a bollocking. But no, he had a surprise for me. 'Tonight,' he said, 'we're playing Liverpool at Upton Park. I want to try you up front.' We won 1–0. After 90 minutes I came off the field with my shorts absolutely wringing wet from the sweat off my fat arse. But it was a liberation, as well as a conversion. Until then I'd been an old-fashioned wing half. It's a position that doesn't exist any more and involves a lot of tackling and marking and kicking the shit out of people. It's quite a boring job to commit to for 15 years. There's something in my character that was more suited to being a front player, having a go, chasing and scoring. Ron had the vision to spot that. I asked him a few weeks later why he'd decided to move me up front. He said, 'When you played in the midfield you liked getting forward but you didn't like getting back.'

Had I not been shovelled up front, who knows what would have happened? My football just took off. Even when adapting to a new role and not yet fit, I had such an outstanding start, scoring 14 goals in 27 games, that I realised something had to give. I had found my calling as a sportsman. It was playing up front for West Ham United. The pipedream of batting in the middle order for Essex vanished in an instant. A striker was born, and cricket was firmly relegated to second place. I won't say it went out the window altogether, because I see from my scrapbook that I was still opening for Chelmsford the following summer. One cutting has me scoring an undefeated 115 in under two hours. 'It was a somewhat restrained innings by Hurst standards,' says the report.

When I think of that era now, I call them the medieval days. The description doesn't feel too far-fetched. Take the most obvious difference. These days there are cameras filming the game from every angle. Referees don't need eyes in the back of their head any more. The cameras can show them and us what happened, in an instant. You can watch the pattern of a move from an overhead cam, see the ball blasting into the net from the behind-the-net cam. Now, there would be a camera in the stanchion of the goalpost that could have determined if my second goal against West Germany really was a goal. The argument would be settled by technology, there and then, and my life might have turned out very differently.

Nowadays we take for granted that every game is served up to us on a platter. Everything is televised on one channel or another. It's an all-you-can-eat buffet of football football football. As the manager of Arsenal, Arsène Wenger used to spend all his free time watching games from all over Europe, studying the way football was being played in Serie A, checking on the form of a prospect in the Bundesliga. Alf Ramsey was a great student of the game, and an innovative tactician. As a club manager at Ipswich he was astute in recruiting a team that could overcome more talented sides. As England manager he spent three years sifting through players, working out who he could rely on. But he had to do almost all of it without access to any of those channels now at everyone's fingertips.

When I began playing football, very little of it reached the living room. The FA Cup final was an annual treat. The odd international was broadcast. Sure, you could read detailed match reports in the papers and you could listen to action on the radio. But you had to take it on trust that such and such a player was a budding superstar. Instead, fans went to the grounds in massive numbers and knew their own team intimately. The only time they clapped eyes on the stars of other clubs was when they visited once a year, or if they drew them in the Cup. When *Match of the Day* was first broadcast at the start of 1964–5, there were fewer people watching highlights from Anfield – a mere 20,000 – than there were spectators attending the actual game.

For years, it's been possible to watch the rise of a young English player from their first kick in the Premier League. Think of Alan Shearer's hattrick on his full debut for Southampton in 1988, or Wayne Rooney's explosive first goal for Everton aged only 16 in 2002, or Marcus Rashford's game-changing brace for Manchester United in 2016. From then on, nothing they ever achieved was a complete surprise. They were known quantities at a young age. Back in the early 1960s, the nation knew Jimmy Greaves by reputation. He was just about the most famous footballer in Europe. But there were no showreels or compilations to verify what we were told. To know for sure how good players were, you had to be there.

That is why there is such a mystique surrounding Duncan Edwards. When I was in my teens he was the unstoppable rising star at Old Trafford. But at the age of 21 his life was cut short by the Munich air crash in 1958. It's one of the big what-ifs of English football. He would certainly have become a very great player, if not the greatest. He had already played 18 times for England, and no one doubts that he would have been in Alf's team in 1966, probably as captain. Bobby Charlton always marvelled at the memory of his brilliance. He could do everything.

The strange thing is, I never saw Duncan Edwards play. I barely ever saw him on television. The cameras weren't there for his every game, and the crumbling footage of him that survives is in grainy black and white. His nearest modern equivalent must be Jude Bellingham. Imagine never having seen Jude Bellingham. It's unthinkable.

If we knew little about English players, we knew far less about foreign players. And they genuinely seemed more foreign in those days, as the deluge bringing the best of the world's talent to the Premier League was still decades away. When I started at West Ham, the only foreign footballer of note to play in England was Bert Trautmann, the German goalkeeper of Manchester City. British players had started to play in Italy. The first foreign team to really capture my imagination were the Hungarians who came to the Empire Stadium, as Wembley was known back then, in 1953 and became the first overseas visitors to beat England. That 6–3 drubbing introduced the lightning speed of the striker Nándor Hidegkuti, who lashed in the first goal after 45 seconds, and the silky skills of Ferenc Puskás, who scored the second with an outrageous drag back that made a fool out of England's captain Billy Wright. No one was doing drag backs in 1953. That display got my attention. Seven years later, my obsession with Puskás's genius went to another level when I saw him and Alfredo Di Stéfano playing up front for Real Madrid in the European Cup final. Together they destroyed Eintracht Frankfurt to the tune of 7–3, winning the ultimate club competition for the fifth season in a row. I hadn't known football could be played with that level of skill.

I first played against foreign teams when Ron Greenwood entered West Ham in a competition called the American International Soccer League held in New York in the summer of 1963. In a four-engine plane we flew for 13 hours via Prestwick to Idlewild – John F. Kennedy, after whom the airport was later named, was yet to be assassinated. New York was brilliant, though with a tight per diem we weren't exactly out nightclubbing. We trained in Central Park and the games took place on Randall's Island. Our group included teams from Brazil, Mexico,

France and West Germany. It was an incredible education. I'd started the season playing cricket for Essex, then struggled in West Ham's reserves. By the end of it, aged 21, I was suddenly playing football against top teams from other countries. I scored a hatful, often in 90°F heat. Against Valenciennes, the match report has me down as a 'goalscoring, all-action hero' with 'massive shooting power'. One left-foot 25-yarder ripped a hole in the back of the net. Blimey, it makes me sound like Popeye. I finished top scorer. Mooro and Martin also profited from the experience. It sounds insignificant, but it was a wholly new thing to hear so many different languages spoken on a football pitch.

Having won our group, we flew home then came back three weeks later to play Górnik Zabrze of Poland, the winners of the other group, in a two-legged final. I put us ahead in the second leg. Then the Scottish referee swiftly disallowed two Górnik goals, prompting 500 Polish New Yorkers to invade the pitch. According to a report in my scrapbook, they 'kicked and pummelled him as police vainly tried to break through', ripped his shirt and smashed his front teeth. Ron took us off the pitch for 20 minutes while 100 NYPD officers restored order with batons. A linesman reffed the rest of the match.

Winning it qualified us to play the previous year's winners over two legs in Chicago and New York. Dukla Prague were run by the Czechoslovak army and among their ranks was Josef Masopust. The previous season he'd won European Footballer of the Year. In the 1962 World Cup in Chile he opened the scoring in the final against Brazil by making a canny late run into the box. So I was on the pitch with someone who'd not just played in a World Cup final, like four of his teammates, but got on the scoresheet. At that point, you could have got extremely long odds on three Hammers playing in the next World Cup final and scoring all four of England's goals. We didn't win, but Masopust was impressed enough to predict that West Ham would be world class within two years.

That experience stood us in good stead the following season. Having won the FA Cup, we qualified to take part in the European Cup Winners' Cup. Over home and away legs we beat Ghent, Spartak Prague, Lausanne Sports and Real Zaragoza before meeting Munich 1860 in the final at Wembley in May 1965. Believe it or not, before Franz Beckenbauer helped turn Bayern into the major force they became, Munich 1860 were then the city's bigger club. But I don't reckon I could have picked any of their players out of a police line-up.

The reality is that, representing either club or country, we wouldn't have been familiar with most of the players we might come up against. The obvious exceptions were Brazil, but in 1966 they didn't make it out of their group so we never faced them. When we met Argentina in the quarter-final, they were not total strangers to most of the team, who had played against them in the so-called Little World Cup in Brazil two years earlier. In the semi-final, too, Eusébio's reputation went before him. Nobby Stiles and Bobby Charlton had played against his club Benfica in the quarter-final of the European Cup only a few months earlier.

But in the main, we were playing against strangers. Without television, there was no chance to get to know them. Even during the World Cup itself there was little opportunity to do homework on opposing teams. We watched some games in the

TV lounge but you had to be concentrating hard to pick up useful details about individuals and playing styles. There were no replays, graphics or statistics, and punditry was in its infancy.

Then there were the playing conditions. These truly were medieval. At West Ham's training ground there would be a sign on the pitch saying KEEP OFF THE GRASS. By late September, there would be no grass to keep off. The only way you could tell there was any sort of pitch was the two goals and the four corner flags. The pitches in the actual grounds were no better. Watching clips from the 1960s, it's a wonder anyone played any football at all. There was no decent drainage back then. The pitch may resemble a bowling green in August but by midwinter it looked like the Somme. We played on mud patches and quagmires, cow pastures and paddy fields. Even the pitch at Wembley could cut up like Aintree on Grand National day.

The ball was different too. The modern football may have many different designs, but it is otherwise uniform in weight and air pressure. The old ball wasn't quite a pig's bladder, but it was made of absorbent unlacquered leather that when wet would get heavier. We'll get on to the implications of that in a later chapter. And in these adverse working conditions, we played many more games per season than any professional would today. Because we'd got to a European semi-final and a domestic cup final, by the time West Ham's players appeared in the World Cup final we should by rights have been ready for the knacker's yard. The final was Bobby Moore's 72nd game of the 1965–6 season. It was Martin Peters's 68th, and my 67th.

The fixture list could sometimes get so crowded that there would be clashes between club and country. In 1965, Nobby was first called up to play for England Under 23s, which meant he would have to miss an important league match for Manchester United. He felt torn between his loyalty to his club and his ambition to catch the eye of Alf Ramsey. His wife Kay stiffened his spine and he plucked up the courage to tell his manager Matt Busby of his choice. As he describes the brief conversation in his autobiography, Busby's response was chilly. Faced with a similar issue, Gordon Banks came up with an unusual solution. In 1961 he was called into the England squad for the first time. The occasion was a midweek international against Portugal. He knew he wouldn't be playing – the first choice was Ron Springett – but he was delighted. His delight turned to dismay when he saw that on the same evening his club Leicester were at home to Atlético Madrid in the Cup Winners' Cup. Oops. Rather than choose between club and country, Banksy worked out that straight after the game he could drive like the clappers from Wembley to Filbert Street. He and his Ford van made it with half an hour to spare.

I admit that in one sense the football has improved. Nowadays everyone gets to play twinkle-toed fast-reaction one-touch stuff on nail-clippered pitches fit for a royal garden party. With a reliable ball on a smooth pitch, and greater science applied to fitness and diet, footballers are able to achieve levels of skill, speed and fitness that were not always possible in the medieval days. My pre-match fuel used to be steak before I wised up and went for more digestible stuff like fried egg and beans on toast.

So it's easy to assume that football now is simply better than football then. I can imagine kids watching the World Cup final I played in and judging it harshly. It can look slower. It's in black and white. Was Bobby Charlton really that good? Or Uwe Seeler?

Yes. They really were. I am here to tell you, a messenger from football's past, that they were fantastic players.

I'm not so sure that football has necessarily had an upgrade. In fact, I would say that the game we played was not just as good, in many respects it was better. It's a physical game, and back then there was a lot more acceptance that you tackled hard but you played fair. I'm not saying it was all exemplary. The FA Cup final replay between Leeds and Chelsea in 1970 is the ultimate video nasty. There was only one booking in the whole game. It's thought that about ten players would have been sent off if the game were played now. It would have ended up five-a-side. Jack Charlton bundling Peter Osgood to the turf like a WWF wrestler? Good God! A few weeks later they were in the same England squad bound for the Mexico World Cup.

So yes, the game could certainly be vicious. In 1966 referees turned a blind eye to some terrible stuff, especially when Pelé was playing for Brazil in the group games. He was basically fouled out of the competition. It sometimes felt like a player had to be the victim of grievous bodily harm to earn a free kick. You could argue that Nobby got away with a very bad foul in the group game against France, and the referee totally lost control of Argentina in our quarter-final. Ours was the last World Cup with no substitutes, though they'd been introduced in friendlies, so the more unscrupulous and violent teams could gain a numerical advantage at no cost.

That said, a lot of the games I watch today are frankly boring. They're too namby-pamby, and they're badly marred by gamesmanship. The sight of players diving to gain an advantage – to get a foul or win a penalty – is absolutely disgraceful. You see it all over world football. It was starting to creep in towards the end of my career, but no one had a reputation for diving or for wasting time. If you were tackled and knocked over, the typical attitude was to get up and show that you weren't hurt, that you weren't going to succumb to intimidation. You didn't roll over three or four times when someone tapped your ankle; and now, as soon as they don't get the foul they were playing for, they're straight up and running back, the feigned injury gone and forgotten. It's a joke. As for prompting the referee to shower the opposition with bookings, don't get me started. I honestly don't know how some modern players can look at themselves in the mirror. Our ethos was closer to that of modern rugby players. You just can't imagine a team in the sixties playing against a team today, falling over with a hand clutched to their throat or face when they've taken a soft elbow to the shoulder. It would be like playing against aliens.

Then there's the money and the status. Stratospheric salaries have opened up a huge gap between the players and the fans whose season tickets and TV subscriptions pay their wages. That gap was nowhere near as wide in my day. I liked it that way, which is why I have never been envious of those who would earn much bigger money. In real terms, Premier League footballers make more in a week than professionals of my era would earn in a year. The top end drags up the bottom end so that nowadays there are some very ordinary players who are earning a fortune. Good luck to them!

But what is interesting to me is how players were perceived within society began to shift over the course of my career. The cap on the maximum wage was removed in 1961. That cap was £20 a week in the season, and £16 over the close season. Steadily the money started to go up. By the time I got into the England squad, I was on £90 a week. After the World Cup, it went up to £140, if on a lock-tight six-year contract.

As a result, players could afford to buy their own homes. When I first started, they often rented a house owned by the club, and when that player was sold, or their career finished, they were evicted. Judith and I bought our first home in 1964, for £5,000. With a mortgage of £3,500, it felt like we'd taken leave of our senses. By the late 1960s we were doing OK financially and so in 1968 we decided to invest in something bigger and more expensive. We found a house in Chigwell, Essex, on a road called Meadow Way, which a Conservative MP had put on the market. Before we'd exchanged contracts and moved in, the news somehow got back to Ron Greenwood. I went to training one day and Ron asked to speak to me privately.

'I gather you're moving into Meadow Way,' he said.

I confirmed that we were.

'The vice chairman lives at the bottom of the road,' he said. 'The chairman and I don't think it's very appropriate that you live in the same road as the vice chairman.'

I now realise that I was part of the great sweep of the sixties, when the barriers between the classes were breaking down as never before. By becoming a neighbour of someone on the board, the player seemed to be claiming he was equal to the paymaster, the worker on a level with the boss. The people at the top didn't like that. I listened to what Ron had to say and, very politely and not in as many words, I told him where to get off.

7

MEETING ALF

'Dear Geoff ...'

As I began working on this book I received a letter from Colchester. It was written by someone who was in one of the years below me.

'I remember you when I was at Rainsford school in Chelmsford,' he says.

I'm quoting it here not to tell you how marvellous I think I am, but it illustrates the way one other person seemed to perceive me back then.

'You were head boy and very clever.'

Ha!

'At morning assembly they would have you up on stage and hold you up as an example to us all.'

Needless to say, I do not remember this. But then he gets personal and recalls a personal tragedy he suffered in 1958.

'You kept an eye on me, thank you.'

I'm quoting this letter because I think it might say something about how I came to play for England in the World Cup. People say to me, 'What impact did Alf Ramsey have on your life?' 'He changed it,' I reply. 'He picked me for England.'

Really, it's as simple as that. In a sense there's not much more to say. I didn't have long conversations with him, and

I would think that applies to everyone else in the team too. Whatever he said or didn't say is relatively unimportant compared to what he did for me. Here I am talking about him 60 years on, but he picked me for a reason, and I suspect it went beyond an ability to score goals. What Alf searched for when he was casting about for 11 good men and true was team players. He wanted footballers who would literally embody the concept of being a teammate.

I must have caught his attention when West Ham had two games against Ipswich in the Easter programme of 1963. Alf was already the national manager, but had chosen to stay on in his club job till the end of the season. In one of them I scored the winner.

A report in my scrapbook suggests that I came up against another Alf team a few weeks later when England had a game against a Football League XI. This one's a curio. The English Football League had been playing the odd match against other representative XIs since the 19th century. Almost all of those games were against the Scottish or Northern Irish equivalent. They only ever played against England once, at Highbury, on 24 May 1963. I find it quite embarrassing that I can recall absolutely nothing about this match: not just what happened in it, but that it happened at all. According to my clipping, selected to play up front for the Football League were Hurst and Hunt. In other words, this was the first time I was paired with Roger. I'd have to wait three years for it to happen again. On top of that, we both scored, Roger on 25 minutes, 'when Dobson walked through an Armfield tackle', me on 34 'after a blunder by Maurice Norman and Ray Wilson'. You'd think I might remember! Of the 22 on the pitch, half would be in Alf's World Cup squad. Just four would play in the final.

I don't remember meeting Alf for another 18 months. I'd already played a few times for the Under 23s when, in November 1964, we assembled to face Wales in Wrexham. The squad members based in the south met at Paddington to travel there by train. Alf came with us and on the way up he was full of questions about people I'd played against. It was more like an interrogation than a friendly chat. I guess this was all part of his process of gathering information. I didn't feel it was my role to ask questions as well as answer them – and I certainly didn't have the confidence to do so. So I found out next to nothing about Alf. Nonetheless, this was probably the longest exchange I ever had with him. Thinking about it now, it occurs to me that perhaps he was attempting to find out what I was like as a person, making an assessment of my character. If I'd come across as a cocky young so-and-so, he might have marked me down as someone who might let him down on the pitch.

Just over a year later, when I joined my first senior squad and I got a longer look at him, my impression didn't change. On the training pitch that first morning he asked for a volunteer and, when I didn't step forward, he had a quiet word in my ear. 'I've no use for blushing violets.' He seemed very disciplined, and very tough. But he didn't allow you to get to know him. Alf wasn't one of those managers who holds loads of big team meetings in which he talks the hind leg off a donkey. In the training sessions, he wouldn't barge onto the field and start telling us what we should do. He'd not be on the touchline shouting and screaming. My sense is that he let us get on with it.

So you were never really sure what he was thinking, or even who he was. He wore a cloak of formality, always addressing us as 'Gentlemen'. No one called me 'Geoffrey'. Alf did. He also called Mooro 'Robert' and Nobby 'Norbert'. This is just a theory, but perhaps it was his way of telling us working-class boys that he'd bettered himself. You'd never have guessed that Alf grew up in Dagenham. He didn't sound anything like Jimmy Greaves, who came from Dagenham too. He had kicked over every single trace of the accent he grew up with.

Along with the clipped voice went the wardrobe of a trust-worthy bank manager. When he wasn't wearing a tracksuit, Alf was usually in a three-piece suit. For the World Cup final, he wore the odd combination of tracksuit and black leather shoes. The most unusual thing about him was his passion for west-erns. Alf was always the one who picked the entertainment, both in the hotel or when we went out, and on almost every occasion he'd plump for a western. He obviously liked cowboys. It could have been worse. If Alf said he was a Donald Duck fan or wanted to watch Mickey Mouse comedies, we'd have sat through them. Reluctantly, perhaps, but you wouldn't complain because you knew that it might be detrimental to your chances of being picked.

In retrospect, the eye-popping prediction he made at the beginning of his first full season as England manager looks very uncharacteristic. 'I believe we will win the World Cup in 1966,' he told the press in August 1963. 'We have the ability. We have the determination. We have the strength. We have the person-ality. We have the character. And we have the players with the temperament. We are just starting to build. I shall go on building up a pool of England players, adding here, discovering there, until I find the final pool for the World Cup.'

That's how the quote was reported in the papers. I remember being surprised at the time. And it wasn't even the first time he'd said it. 'With four or five or six of today's players,' he suggested earlier in the summer after a draw with Brazil, 'I hope it will be possible to find a team good enough to win the World Cup.' The team that day included Gordon Banks, Ray Wilson, Bobby Moore, Bobby Charlton and Jimmy Greaves.

Perhaps Alf really did believe in himself that much. After all, his career in club management suggested he could work wonders. When he took over at Ipswich Town in 1955, the club was in the Third Division South. (Back then there was a geographical split between the two lower professional leagues.) Ipswich was a footballing backwater. Within two seasons of Alf's arrival they'd won the Third Division South title. In another four they'd won the Second Division.

What happened next still looks unbelievable more than 60 years later. Sending out a team with no outstanding players, and straight after being promoted, Alf won the First Division in 1961–2. Their style was the opposite of the football Ron Greenwood was developing at West Ham. We played attractive open stuff that was well suited to knockout competitions but got us nowhere in the league. Alf's Ipswich team were pragmatists who made themselves hard to beat. 'You'll go there and dominate 89 minutes of the play,' Ray Wilson told Bobby Charlton, 'and still lose.' Granted, this was in the period when the league championship was a healthy democracy and the title was passed around much more widely than it is among today's super-rich mega-clubs. But still, as unlikely fairytale champions, Ipswich stand comparison with Brian Clough's Nottingham Forest, who also won it straight after promotion in 1977–8, and of course with Leicester City, who by some miracle managed to win the Premier League under Claudio Ranieri in 2015–16.

Although Alf wasn't the FA's first choice, that title win got him the England job. The first thing he did was tell the suits at the FA that the established practice of selecting the England team by committee had to go. His team, his rules, his responsibility. Alf basically said, *If you want me to be in charge then that's what I'll be. It's my team now and you can fuck off out of it.* He did like to swear now and then, though probably not in this particular meeting. When he won that battle, he must have felt invincible.

He knew how to pick a team, and he knew the sort of player he liked. Hence the prediction. It was only later, when I got to be around him, that the prediction puzzled me. It just didn't sound like the sort of statement that would come from Alf. His instinct was to keep his cards close to his chest, and he didn't like giving journalists anything if he could get away with it.

So I've sometimes wondered why on earth Alf gave the press this stick to beat him with. Imagine any manager in any competition saying, 'We're going to win it.' Fans may chant, 'We're gonna win the league,' but managers don't offer hostages to fortune like that. I remember when Scotland qualified for the World Cup in 1978 (and England didn't). Led by their manager Ally MacLeod, they set off for Argentina like conquering heroes with the sounds of a catchy single called 'Ally's Tartan Army' by Andy Cameron ringing in their ears. The chorus seemed pretty certain of what would happen out there: 'And we'll really shake them up / When we win the World Cup / 'Cause Scotland are the greatest football team.' Much as I love the Scots, the fanfare was all a bit ridiculous. They didn't get out of their group. I wonder whether that song – and the great burden of expectation it brought with it – ate away at the players.

That said, not for a second do I think Alf's forecast weighed on the players. We may have thought it was a crazy thing to say. But you can only go out and do what you do and play like you play.

I first clapped eyes on Alf before I would have been really aware of him. He was a right back at Tottenham but as league games weren't televised in those days I only caught sight of him when he played for England. He earned 32 caps between 1948 and 1953. He was on the pitch for two of the most momentous defeats in the history of English football. I was too young to see England somehow manage to lose 1–0 to the USA in 1950. It was the first World Cup we had bothered to enter and our team included great stars of the era: Billy Wright, Wilf Mannion, Tom Finney, Stan Mortensen. They were names to conjure with and yet on a bumpy pitch in Belo Horizonte, almost by accident these giants of the game were beaten by a bunch of American amateurs.

No one was more mortified than Alf. But worse was to come when Hungary paid their famous visit to the Empire Stadium three years later. By now I was almost 12. I saw the highlights on television and was thrilled by the sight of the Mighty Magyars pinging the ball around as if playing football from the future. Bobby Moore was watching too and, at the final whistle, he literally didn't believe the 6–3 scoreline.

It was a demonstration. Their skills were out of this world. Stanley Matthews, who was 38, was among those the Hungarians ran rings round. The Magyars were far younger and nippier. The spectacular Hidegkuti was the oldest at 31. Alf was nearly 34. He scored the last goal of the game from the penalty spot. He never played for England again.

'Perhaps England, once the masters, can now learn from the pupils,' said Ferenc Puskás after the game. No one learned like Alf. Some players can absorb these traumas and move on. I suspect I would have done. My character is to take things in my stride. I don't get overexcited or terribly depressed. But Alf still seemed to bear the psychological scars deep within him when he took over as England manager a decade later. You could argue that the team he created for the World Cup was a product of that humbling. If he could help it, no team of Alf's was going to be torn apart quite so savagely. 'Even in the days when England had great players like Stanley Matthews, Tom Finney and Raich Carter,' he said when he was appointed, 'the team would have been better with a rigid plan. Any plan must be adapted to the strengths and weaknesses of the players.' It explains why the first building blocks to be put in place for the 1966 team were the back five. By the start of the World Cup, Banksy, George, Jack, Mooro and Ray had played together 11 times. Alf's England were never going to ship goals by the half-dozen.

That said, they did let in five in his first game in charge. It was away to France in Paris, in February 1963. I'm not going to claim I was paying much attention, because I probably wasn't, but this was a significant period for Bobby Moore. The new captain was Jimmy Armfield, but he was injured for the summer tour and Alf gave the armband to Mooro. He had just 11 caps, and he was only 22.

England fans who suffered through the seventies and eighties, not to mention the noughties, will know what it feels like when the national side underachieves. What people may not understand is that this was how it was up until Alf took over too. 'The aim is to win the 1958 World Cup,' said manager Walter Winterbottom. They didn't get out of their group. In 1962, they were soundly beaten in the quarter-final. Brazil, starring Pelé, won both tournaments.

So why did it work for Alf when it didn't for his predecessor or any of his successors?

The first thing to say is that he was all about trust. Alf needed to feel he could rely on the men he picked. Over those three years he grew very good at honing the squad down by weeding people out who he thought might let him down by being weak on the pitch or making wrong decisions, by not working hard enough or not playing for the team. He wanted team players rather than soloists. He had to find 11 of them, and preferably more.

There were two things Alf said to pretty much every player. When I joined the squad for the first time, he told me he didn't expect me to do anything that I hadn't already been doing for my club. This was about building confidence. Later, once I was established and felt part of the England set-up, I left the team hotel after one game and said to Alf, 'See you next time.' 'If selected, Geoffrey.' It turns out he said that to all the boys. This was about ensuring confidence didn't become over-confidence.

Even the 22 he did pick for 1966 included players who he seemed to have his doubts about. As for the ones who didn't make it, I won't pick anyone out by name, but there were some quite big players who you thought might be in the team or the squad who weren't. Years later, as I got to know them socially, senior players like Bobby Charlton and Ray Wilson would confide that such and such player was never going to be picked again because he had somehow or other blotted his copybook. It could be something as seemingly minor as being late for dinner. Back then discipline in wider society was still very strict, and it certainly was with Alf. Players who didn't want to adhere to it were not selected again.

The most obvious restraint he placed on the players was to do with drink. At night, Les Cocker and Harold Shepherdson, Alf's trainer and physio, would prowl the corridors like prison guards, making sure no one nipped out for a swift pint or three. Even though it was possible to have a softer relationship with Alf's two assistants, they formed an unbreakable trio. They were the bosses and we were the workers.

I wasn't there for the most notorious example of Alf's disciplinarianism, but the story was soon known to anyone who was selected to play for England. In 1964, just before the squad flew out on tour, Alf let the players go out for a drink in the West End but imposed a half-ten curfew. A few players missed it – by an hour, or much more, depending on which version of the story you read. Among them were Mooro, Jimmy, Ray, Banksy and Bobby. When they got back to their rooms each found his passport resting on his pillow. Is this where Francis Ford Coppola got the idea for the horse's head in *The Godfather*? Those five, all of them world class, were obviously indispens-able. But it was a shock, and the message went in. It was a

Playing cricket for Essex Schoolboys. My first time being captained by Mooro.

Wives and girlfriends of the 1964 FA Cup winners: Tina Moore stands on the right, and my fiancée Judith sits second from right.

Martin Peters bats for England at our training camp in Roehampton.

Jimmy Greaves shows his pace at pre-tournament boot camp in Lilleshall.

After the draw with Uruguay, Alf took the squad to Pinewood to meet the likes of Yul Brynner and Sean Connery.

The quarter-final against Argentina was the nastiest game any of us ever played for England.

My near-post header that beat Argentina was made on West Ham's training ground …

… and Bally, the most passionate footballer I've ever met, leapt into my arms.

The 1966 squad with trainer Les Cocker (left) and physio Harold Shepherdson (right). No idea why I'm sitting in the middle!

We're in the final. England after beating Portugal in the semi …

… with two goals from Bobby Charlton, here congratulated by Eusébio.

I'm still in the middle in this one. Note the captain striking his favourite pose.

The night before the final, Alan Ball's fiancée Lesley, Judith, Kay Stiles, Norma Charlton, Pat Wilson, Carol Paine and Ursula Banks were snapped on their way to *The Black and White Minstrel Show*.

Early lunch on the day of the final. My selection ahead of Jimmy made me the story, which may be why I am looking at the camera.

The final. As the teams line up, Mooro makes his secret signal to his wife Tina in the stands.

Making sure keeper Hans Tilkowski knows I'm there. Perfectly legal in 1966!

The feeling of scoring
in the final shows
in my embarrassing
celebration: I have
arrived. 1–1.

I was unsighted, but
Roger's reaction has
always been good
enough for me. It was
over the line. 3–2.

My father patiently
taught me to use my
left foot. It worked. 4–2.

It is now. Banksy, Mooro, Roger and me after the final whistle.

After the final, Jimmy slipped away on holiday. 'A touch of the Greta Garbos,' he called it.

Alf is waiting to greet us before we head up the 39 steps.

warning intended to freeze the blood of all mavericks. The other thing that's telling about the story is that Alf had those passports in the first place. Clearly he didn't trust players to look after their own documents.

The memory of it must have faded by the time Alan Ball and Nobby Stiles joined the squad in 1965. In the training camp at Lilleshall before the World Cup, they did something similar. Alf read them the riot act. Bally and Nobby were contrite. John Connelly, who'd been in and out of the squad since 1959, had been out with them and tried to argue that a pint after training was surely acceptable. According to Nobby, he even swore. 'We are here for a purpose,' Alf told us in training the next day. 'I just want to say that if anyone gets the idea of popping out for a pint, then they will be finished with the squad forever.'

Nobby was so spooked by the incident that he abandoned all thought of asking for leave to return to Manchester for the birth of his second child. This was before fathers routinely attended births – Pat Charlton was near full term during the World Cup and you can't imagine Jack itching to get back to home to be in the delivery suite. Nobby was a bit more progressive but he'd got the hint. Alf liked to pretend the players didn't have private lives away from football. Alan Hinton once missed his wedding night to join up with the squad but, instead of being rewarded, he was barely ever to be selected again. Nobby got the message. 'You must be joking!' he said to his heavily pregnant wife Kay when the idea of attending the birth came up.

Nobby and Bally kept a vow of silence about the incident for years, and didn't even tell their wives till Bally let it slip one night in 2002 when they were all dining together. Both became central to Alf's plans. John Connelly played only once more for England. Jack at least had the wisdom to seek permission to go out for a pint. 'No, Jack,' Alf would say after pretending to consider the request, 'I don't think so.' As for myself, luckily I was quite a disciplined person. I found it easy to resist the lure of the pub. As a young player who was new to the squad, I didn't want to do anything that might jeopardise my chance of selection. I was there to get picked, not pissed.

In effect, Alf's selection policy was like Moneyball before Moneyball. As he famously said to Jack, 'I don't always pick the best players, you know.' It was important to fit in with his plan, and for that he went for hard-nosed pros who he absolutely knew, based on solid evidence, could do a job for him. Ours was a team with no weak link. There wasn't one person of whom he could say, 'I'm not sure about him.'

I had never expected to be one of them. You could have knocked me over with a feather when Ron Greenwood took me aside three days before Christmas in 1965 and told me I was in the senior squad. But once there, I just understood that Alf was picking me for the way I played for my club, and that was how he wanted me to play for England, if selected. Ron even said as much: 'the way you train and behave and play for West Ham is exactly what you should be doing for England'. To have that advice was fantastic.

I took heart from what I knew about the way Alf set up his team at Ipswich. He favoured twin strikers, one of them good in the air. Having seen me play as one half of just such a partnership for West Ham, he obviously thought I could fit in with his strategy. He'd already tried plenty of forwards.

Among them were Fred Pickering, Frank Wignall, Mick Jones, Barry Bridges, Joe Baker, Alan Peacock and my old West Ham teammate Johnny Byrne. Not all those names may ring much of a bell nowadays. They were good players, but some got injured and others fell out of favour with their clubs or for some reason didn't quite appeal to Alf. And there are one or two others from the era who were good enough to be selected but never got the call.

You can't say I didn't time my run well. Although I didn't play, the first international where I joined the squad was in Liverpool against Poland on 5 January 1966. The following day, at the Royal Garden Hotel in Kensington, the draw was held for the World Cup.

It was at Lilleshall, where we spent a couple of weeks training, that Alf made his last selection before the tournament began. There were 27 of us (in fact, 28, but Brian Labone of Everton, though he trained with us, had been given the all-clear by Alf to have the summer off to get married). Five of us weren't going to make it into the 22, and competition was aggressive. I had only just got in the team and I had no guarantee at all that I would be in the 22. We were all fighting. Our days there were planned out from nine in the morning till nine at night: fitness sessions, practice matches, drills, films on football, plus a bit of mucking about with cricket and golf and the obligatory westerns by way of relaxation. Just to increase the boot-camp aura, we slept in dormitories.

'The programme we planned was murder,' said our physio Harold Shepherdson. 'I felt sorry for the lads.' The routines would involve a lot of individual running, the length of the pitch backwards and forwards, racing against one another. The quickest was Bobby Charlton. I remember Terry Paine and Ian Callaghan were also quite rapid. Mooro's speed was all in his head so he was one of the slower ones. When distance was involved, so was Jimmy. It was clear we weren't messing about. That bunch of players wanted to get into the squad. So the five-a-sides and 11-a-sides were very, very tough. Even Nobby, who was the toughest of us, was struck by how physical you had to be in games against your mates. The tackling was so aggressive you easily could have injured someone, but you didn't want to be seen to be shirking. Alf would be liable to say, 'He's pulled out of that, send him home.' Even Mooro worked up a sweat. We all knew he was not a candidate to be dropped but he didn't train like that. My memory is that it was probably safer going into a challenge with him than with Jack. I knew Mooro, who wasn't quite as physically ruthless, might be slightly nicer to me. Jack certainly wouldn't have been.

When the selection was made, and five players were sent home, the rest of us went on a four-match tour of Scandinavia and Poland. I didn't perform that well in the game against Denmark. The day before, we did quite a lot of strenuous exercises which I felt were too heavy even for me, and I felt slightly hampered. Then Jimmy got four against Norway and Roger got two goals in the four games while I got none. So I was not surprised when Alf picked those two ahead of me for all of the group games. I was just delighted to be there.

Alf's team came to be known as the Wingless Wonders but it took him a long time to lose faith in the old-school way of playing. Wingers had been an important part of the English game for a very long time. The great English icons Finney and Matthews played the English way, dribbling down the touch-line, beating the full back and crossing to the far post. Alf had four wingers in the provisional squad, but when he whittled it down, only Peter Thompson of Liverpool was culled. Any armchair pundit would suppose that Alf was wary of deviating from tradition.

The problem with wingers was that they didn't contribute much else. They weren't really programmed to defend, or do any of the heavy lifting in midfield. And yet there were as many wingers as strikers in the World Cup squad. In the group games Alf tried all of them. John Connelly had a go at unpicking the Uruguayan defence. Then Terry Paine was asked to do the same against Mexico. When he sustained concussion, Ian Callaghan was given a chance against France.

Then came the quarter-final against Argentina, when Alf took a brave tactical gamble. He knew his England could prosper without wings, because he had done so in masterminding a famous win in Madrid at the end of 1965. Finding that they had no one to mark had completely messed with the heads of Spain's full backs. For some reason, Alf went straight back to the old way of playing and the Wingless Wonders weren't seen again. One theory is that he didn't want to give too much away before the World Cup. Another is that he just got lucky and stumbled on the formula. Either way, it was a major decision, and a major transformation. He now fielded almost the same team that had beaten Spain. There were two new faces. One was Martin Peters. The other, playing in the World Cup for the first time, was me.

An awful lot has been written about England v. Argentina. Our opponents came into the tournament with a dark reputation from the previous World Cup, and had promised to be on their best behaviour. 'We shall try to avoid physical contact,' said their new manager Juan Carlos Lorenzo. Then when they had a player sent off against West Germany, he ran onto the pitch to argue with the ref. They were booed in their next game against Switzerland. The heat was rising. 'What we really hope for is a referee who will not be pressured by the Wembley crowd,' Lorenzo said in the run-up to the quarter-final.

I can't remember much in the way of a tactical team talk before the game. Everything was done on an individual basis, but I don't think Alf would have said anything specific to me. He had one main instruction: we must expect to be provoked, but on no account must we retaliate. 'Whatever you do, you have to walk away from everything.' I do remember Alf adding that seven or eight of the team probably didn't need telling. Self-control was more of a stretch for Bally and Nobby and Jack. But they were top-class professional players who were asked to rely on their common sense to get them through.

This was the biggest test for Alf's theory about gathering strong characters. In the cauldron of that game, weaker players would have let Alf down. But they had been weeded out. The Argentines picked the wrong 11 men to spit at.

We soon knew that it was going to be a tough dirty game. Nasty late tackles were being made that we didn't often see at club level. There was one on Martin early on. But we were unafraid. The English league was very tough and it conditioned us not to fear injury. And I had the awareness to be able to look after myself.

I'd played in one very dirty Under 23 game in Tel Aviv against some fairly unscrupulous Israelis, and had met South American clubs in New York three summers earlier. This was my first time playing against a South American national side. The Argentine antics – spitting, pinching cheeks, tapping ankles, tugging hair, tweaking skin, playacting, pulling shirts, twisting ankles when you were on the ground, sticking fingers in eyes, randomly kicking you miles off the ball – were very unusual. My role in the team, and my style of play, probably protected me from the worst of it. I was difficult to mark because I was always on the move. If you're running, chasing, turning defenders back towards their own goal, they can't get close enough to tackle you from behind. So I wasn't easy to mark or to kick or, for that matter, to spit at. I suffered less of the nonsense than Nobby, who was in the engine room and couldn't avoid constant contact with the enemy.

I did sustain a black eye though. These things can happen inadvertently, but I always wondered if it was deliberate. It came at the hands of the captain Antonio Rattín. He was a big lad so it would be quite easy for him to elbow me in the eye. He was a bit like an Exocet missile: you could see him coming but there was bugger all you could do about it.

In the long drawn-out drama of his dismissal for arguing with the referee, it took him seven minutes to go. First he asked for an interpreter. Then the whole team left the pitch in protest and only returned when told they were in danger of forfeiting the tie. Today, you'd have half a dozen from either side getting involved, but all the England players kept their distance. I don't think I ever got nearer than 20 or 30 yards.

The winner when it came was made in Chadwell Heath. Martin took a pass up the left wing from Ray, glanced up and floated an inch-perfect cross round the full back towards the near post. Darting on a diagonal from near the penalty spot, I rose to glance it across the goalkeeper into the far corner. Textbook West Ham. As I threw my arms up, Bally arrived first and, being the most passionate footballer I've ever met, leapt into my arms. Luckily he was a lot smaller than me.

Years later, we would all laugh about the game. Bally used to joke that Rattín was a lovely man. 'He would kick you in the balls but then he would help you look for them.' We would also come to see it as the nastiest game we ever played for England. At the final whistle, the referee left the field under heavy protection while Alf was spitting tacks, disgusted at what he perceived to be conduct unbecoming. He even intervened to prevent George Cohen from swapping shirts with the winger Alberto González. But Alf couldn't get round the whole team. González swapped with Ray instead. And there's a press snap of Bobby with an Argentine opponent: he's already removed his own shirt and handed it over, while the opposition player is leaning towards him so Bobby can delicately peel the white and blue shirt off his back. He always was the politest of us.

The battle continued in the tunnel. The Argentine players were sparring for a fight. I vividly remember them trying to force their way into our dressing room, which was opposite theirs. We heard a bang on the plate-glass window of the door. Someone had hurled a chair at it. On the after-dinner circuit, Banksy used to have fun recalling the brouhaha. He'd paint a picture of Nobby crouching between Jack's legs and shouting,

'Let the bastards in!' Having behaved so well for 90 minutes, those two were certainly up for a fight. Ray was too, reasoning that half of the Argentineans were even shorter than him. The shouting must have gone on for a good quarter of an hour but the door wasn't opened. I wasn't shocked or frightened, and part of me even found it amusing. The police eventually turned up. 'Forget them,' Alf told us. 'You're in the semi-final. They're flying home tomorrow.'

It's in this context that the controversy of Alf's post-match interview on television should be considered. 'We have still to produce our best football,' he said. 'It will come against the right type of opposition, a team who come to play football and not act as animals.' He didn't quite describe the Argentines as animals, he just said they behaved like that. It attracted a torrent of criticism. Later on, I came to see how offence was taken. At the time, not being aware of the politics in FIFA and beyond, I probably didn't understand the significance. After what we'd been subjected to, I thought he was fairly justified.

If it was a mistake, it was the gut reaction of a man who believed in fair play, and in loyally protecting his players. None of us minded. On that day, after three years of all that sifting and sorting, for the first time he fielded 11 men he knew would give him everything.

That night he let us have a drink. And he ordered a stiff one for himself.

8

SWEET FA

Grass doesn't stop growing when you're off winning World Cups. The afternoon after my hattrick, following a stop-off for the team at ATV to appear on a television show hosted by Eamonn Andrews, I went home to Hornchurch and mowed the lawn. I'd been away for many weeks. The grass was so long it didn't just need cutting, it practically needed threshing. Also the car looked like it could use a wash, so I did that too.

As for a lot of the players, there was a slight feeling of emptiness after the euphoria – a vague sense of 'Is that it?' I probably didn't understand at once that this was the first day of the rest of my life. Yes, there was a bit of a hullaballoo when Judith and I went shopping for the first time. We were mobbed and my back got slapped a lot. 'Our lives will never be the same again,' Bobby Charlton said to Jack when they were still on the pitch. The realisation that this was true for me too dawned more gradually. The fundamental change was felt not over days and weeks but through the seasons.

We all came back down to earth at different speeds. Nobby Stiles and Alan Ball drove north together and stopped for fish and chips on the M6. No one requested an autograph, though someone did ask to see Bally's medal. Jack woke up with a throbbing hangover in Leytonstone in the house of a complete stranger. He went out into the back garden and who should be saying hello over the fence but a woman he knew from Ashington, the Northumbrian village where the Charltons grew up? Martin Peters had a more literal prang with reality when he and Kathy were motoring home the next day and someone drove into his rear bumper. It was two of the quietest and shyest members of the team who had the biggest fanfare when they got back. There were banners in the street awaiting Ray Wilson, and Roger Hunt arrived at his front door to be cheered by a spontaneous gathering of hundreds.

For me, there was an overgrown lawn. The story of me and my mower has been mentioned a lot in books and articles. I can see that it's sort of funny, but I've never quite understood what's so noteworthy about performing a couple of regular domestic chores. It's not as if I'd suddenly turned into someone who had his grass cut for him. I suppose it's a symbol of something. On Saturday, you're a superman whose heroics have been seen by an audience of hundreds of millions all around the world. On Sunday, you go into the back garden where real life cuts you down to size.

But we didn't need real life to do that for us. We had the Football Association.

It began with the bonus. The FA had decided to award £22,000 to the squad in the event of victory. It looks like a random figure on one level. Why not £25,000? Hey, why not £50,000? Why not 10 grand a head, such as the Germans were rumoured to be getting for losing? But there were 22 members of the squad so you can see a logic. Then some bright spark – or rather a whole committee of them – thought it would be suitable to give 500 quid to each squad member and then divide the rest according to time spent on the pitch. With this formula, the more a player had played in the tournament, the more he would get. By implication, the less he'd played, the less he'd get. Seven of the squad had played all six games. Seven had played in none. I'll say their names here: Ron Springett, Peter Bonetti, Jimmy Armfield, Gerry Byrne, Ron Flowers, Norman Hunter, George Eastham. In other words, the FA's thoughtless idea was to drive a wedge straight down the middle of the 22. When Alf Ramsey told us about it after the game, without consulting anyone Bobby Moore showed real leadership and proposed – no, he insisted – that the money be shared equally. We had trained together as a squad and those who had not played had been vital to keeping up morale. Alf agreed. A cheque for £1,000 duly arrived with a letter signed by Denis Follows, the secretary of the FA. After tax, a grand went down to around 600 quid. It took another eight years for the Inland Revenue to relent and give us a rebate. Not that we did it for the money. Representing England wasn't a job. It was an honour.

Talking of which, in the New Year Honours list, Follows had his MBE upgraded to a CBE. Later, he was knighted for services to sport. Probably his most honourable achievement in football was to lift the 50-year ban on women's football in 1970. I've got nothing against him personally. But he represents that cadre of sports administrators who have never massively impressed me. And that's just the English ones. I'll get on to the ones from other countries.

Football back then wasn't much different from the class structure in cricket. It was the gentlemen who were in charge, the blazered Corinthian Casuals types with peppery RAF moustaches and a whiff of the Rotary Club. They, the nobs, seemed to look down on us, the yobs. But things were starting to shift. Footballers began to earn a bit more, and the World Cup winners were now going for big money. Straight after the tournament Bally was sold by Blackpool to Everton for £110,000. In 1970, Martin Peters would become the first English player to be transferred for £200,000. Although I didn't find out till much later, I might have broken that record in 1968, but Ron Greenwood turned down Matt Busby's approach in a terse telegram: 'No. Regards, Greenwood.'

But any money players earned on the side had to be done under their own steam. There was no such thing as image rights in those days so when Marks and Spencer brought out a shirt with our faces on them, we didn't get a penny. That was the way it was. I do remember one player perk. In a matchday programme for the World Cup there was an advertisement for a make of raincoat, which was modelled by the squad. By way of payment we all received one raincoat each. There was even a choice of colour. Royal blue or white, or possibly beige. I have a feeling I went for blue.

It was only decades later that we as a collective worked out a way to monetise our achievement.

In 1966, playing football at the highest level did not mean you'd never have to work again. The best you could hope for was to be comfortably off. And then after you finished, you were on your own. The one to fall furthest and fastest was George Cohen. He won his 37th cap for England in November 1967. The next month when playing against Liverpool he twisted his knee agonisingly and sustained bad cartilage damage. He attempted to play on after rehabilitation, but eventually a Harley Street doctor told him his career was over. Ray Wilson's knee did for him too, but more slowly. He played his 63rd and last game for England in the third-place European Championship play-off against the Soviet Union in June 1968. Both our full backs found a career outside football, George in property, Ray in undertaking. Roger Hunt was the only one of us to do things completely on his own terms, retiring from international football in 1969 when he easily could have added to his 34 caps. Eventually he followed George and Ray out of football, joining the family haulage firm.

Winning the World Cup did not immunise us against insult. The greatest blow to a teammate's pride was inflicted on Gordon Banks. Less than a year after our triumph, the best goalkeeper on the planet suffered the humiliation of being dropped by Leicester City and sold to Stoke City for a mere £50,000. They were keen to bring on a talented teenager in the second team called Peter Shilton, who told the club that he'd leave unless he played in the first team. Jimmy Greaves found his way back into the England side in the spring of 1967, but won only three more caps.

My low point didn't arrive until 1972 when Ron decided he no longer needed me at West Ham and Alf made the same decision about my England career. Winning my 49th cap, which like my first was against West Germany, I was substituted in the 58th minute. I remember being very annoyed about this at the time. As the youngest of us, Bally had the longest post-1966 life as an international, eventually winning 72 caps. He was made captain by Don Revie but in 1975, soon after England had thrashed Scotland 5–1, he was ruthlessly dropped. Decades later he was still scratching his head about it.

By the end of the 1970s we'd all retired and those of us who hadn't left football straight away had a crack at management. You might expect our very greatest players, the two Bobbys, to be able to mould teams in their own image, but it's probably true that they weren't ruthless or clinical enough to be the leaders off the pitch that they had been on it. Both would have more impact running football schools, where winning games isn't the yardstick of achievement. Bobby Charlton's one job in management, apart from a very brief spell as caretaker at Wigan, was at Preston North End, where he took on Nobby as his coach. They didn't last long. I can't begin to imagine how humiliating it must have been for Mooro, who by then was strapped for cash after the failure of various business ventures, to have to take a job with Oxford City in 1980. With the greatest respect, Oxford United would have been humbling enough, but Oxford City? It seems extraordinary that no professional club would touch him. Then in 1984 he took charge at Fourth Division Southend United, which I suppose was a step up. That same summer Franz Beckenbauer was appointed to coach West Germany.

It was the earthier and – let's be frank – gobbier members of the team who would be better suited to management. Bally went on to have a lot of jobs in football, but it was Jack Charlton who was best cut out for a career on the other side of the touchline. He was never shy about speaking his mind and he had extremely firm ideas about how to win football matches.

He did well enough in his first job at Middlesbrough that when Revie walked out on England in 1977, Jack thought he'd write to the FA and apply for the vacancy. He never received a reply. Obviously, this was an insult to Jack first and foremost, but the FA's silence also said something about what the men in suits thought of the 1966 team. England's loss would, a decade on, be the Republic of Ireland's gain. Instead, the job fell to Ron Greenwood and he asked me to join his coaching staff. So I became the only one of the 1966 team who would have anything further to do with England.

It was in this role that I discovered the FA top brass also liked to look down on the coaching staff too. The chief culprit was Sir Harold Thompson. He was the ultimate amateur, his sole qualification as a football administrator being a blue he won playing for Oxford University. Later, he taught chemistry there. Alf once had to ask him to stop blowing cigar smoke in the faces of the players. Thompson was instrumental in the brutal sacking of Alf in 1974, and two years later his reward was to be appointed FA chairman. That was when I had more first-hand exposure. I distinctly remember being on the coach with the squad one day. Ron was sitting towards the back and, clambering aboard, Harold Thompson called him 'Greenwood'. It's a mode of address that may have been normal in the corridors of power, but in our world it was totally unheard of and struck me as extremely rude. It was as if he was talking to staff.

Years later, it gave me great pleasure to see Sir Harold get a taste of his own medicine. I was in Hong Kong airport with my wife after doing something at a PR event. We were in the first-class lounge about to fly home when we spotted the great chemist outside at a desk trying to wangle some sort of upgrade. Whatever it was he was after, and however high on his horse he got, the person he was asking looked extremely reluctant to give it to him. I confess that Judith and I both found this extremely amusing.

What I'm describing is a world in which, however great their achievements, footballers of my era were generally not seen by the FA to have equal status. As a result, back then no one had the wit or imagination to think in terms of legacy. We the players were powerful symbols of something that really mattered. But the men in blazers couldn't see it. It remains an absolute scandal that the FA didn't find a way to welcome Mooro into the fold and make him a figurehead. He had such charm and polish he would have made a wonderful ambassador for English football. But our captain, the only Englishman ever to lift the World Cup, was ignored and found a humbler home for himself as a matchday pundit for a local London radio station. Not even a national one!

For a time, West Ham weren't much better. A steward once booted the club captain, who'd lifted the FA Cup and Cup Winners' Cup, out of Upton Park because he didn't have a ticket. He should have been given the freedom of the ground, to sit wherever he wanted. When I first heard that story I would have struggled to believe it. But then I watched a similar thing happen to Ron Greenwood. By then I was working as an ambassador for a double-glazing company, which had signed a sponsorship deal with West Ham. At one game, Ron was in the directors' lounge and I heard he wanted to say hello. I walked along the side of the main stand to greet him and he asked after

Judith. As she was back in the sponsor's lounge, he said he'd go there with me. But first we had to walk through a lounge.

'Have you got tickets?' said this guy on the door.

Ron didn't.

'In that case, I'm afraid you can't come through.'

I looked up above the door and saw that the room to which he was refusing us entry was called the Ron Greenwood Lounge. You couldn't make it up.

And it happened to me too. Except that I couldn't even get into the ground. The sponsorship deal had been announced with a big fanfare. The company boss owned a helicopter, which his pilot landed on the pitch before a game, and out we both stepped, sponsor and ambassador. That was my most public appearance, but I remained heavily involved. Before one Monday night match, for example, I was to be interviewed on the pitch. So I arrived early.

'Have you got a ticket?' said the guy at the main entrance.

'No, I haven't,' I said. 'I'm with the sponsors and I'm sitting with them and doing a piece on the pitch.'

Standing a few yards behind this man on the gate was the commercial manager of the club. The doorman looked around at him for guidance. The commercial manager didn't say anything. He just shook his head. I can still see him doing it now.

This was before mobiles so I couldn't ring anyone up there and then to complain.

It sounds astonishing now but at the time it was fairly common. Footballers were not welcome back at their clubs. Then, I was probably as amused as I was irritated. I just rolled my eyes and got on with it. What good would rage have done me? We all lived with the reality that ex-footballers were not seen to have high status. But when I think about it in more detail now, I feel much more aggrieved. If only it had happened a few years later.

'You see that statue over there?' I could have said.

'Yeah?'

'The two blokes holding up another bloke who's holding a cup, with another standing beside them.'

'Yeah. What of it?'

'That's the World Cup.'

'And?'

'And the bloke who's holding it was captain of England. He's called Bobby Moore. He played 544 times for this club whose gates you are guarding. The one standing to the side is called Martin Peters. He played 302 games for West Ham and scored in the World Cup final. One bloke holding up Mooro is Ray Wilson. Great guy, best left back ever to play for England, but I'll let you off because he wasn't a Hammer.'

'Cheers, mate, thanks for the history lesson.'

'Hang about, I haven't finished. The other bloke holding him up is called Geoff Hurst. He scored 248 goals in 499 games for West Ham, and three goals in the World Cup final. And if you go and have a closer look at the statue, my friend, you'll see he bears a striking similarity to me. Now please will you let me in to my old ground?'

Never happened, sadly. They didn't put the statue up till later. But Judith got her own back on the commercial manager, who came up to the sponsor's box at half time. West Ham were not in a good place that season. 'We could do with you on the pitch today,' he said to me. Judith said, 'Does he need a ticket for that too?' And I did have some belated satisfaction. When he was going for a job interview he had the nerve to ask me for a reference. He didn't get it.

If my fantasy rant makes me sound petty and self-important, all I can say is it compresses into a few words the feelings of disappointment that my teammates and I quietly harboured about the way the memory of what we had achieved together had somehow been allowed to fade. I remember seeing Mooro and Bally go on *Wogan* in 1991 on the 25th anniversary of our win. Between them they made an eloquent argument that the FA should be doing more to mark the moment. Some of us had a meal with some of the Germans, but that was about it.

Perhaps we can't blame football for not cherishing old footballers. Perhaps it reflected something in wider society. I sometimes felt the chill of indifference or worse when I moved into the world of business. This came after the seven years I spent in management, when in 1984 I decided to look for more reliable employment and got a job in insurance. First, I had to go on an induction course. A key component of the job was the ability to open the phonebook, make a cold call and persuade the person on the other end of the line to listen to what you had to offer. My character suited me to the work, which required a level head. So I selected a name and dialled the number. A woman answered.

'Hello, my name's Geoff Hurst,' I said. 'I work for a company called Abbey Life.'

'I don't deal with insurance,' she said. 'My husband deals with it. I'll go and get him.'

After a bit of a wait the husband came on the phone.

'My wife tells me you're Geoff Hurst,' he said.

'That's correct.'

'Well, if you're Geoff Hurst I'm fucking Marilyn Monroe.'

To this day I don't know if he was claiming to be Marilyn – or claiming to be intimate with her.

Now, I've told that story many times. It's a staple of my stage show and it always gets a good reaction. I can see that it is funny to hear a World Cup winner make himself the butt of a joke. How are the mighty fallen, and all that. Also, how times have changed. Bet they wouldn't say that to Harry Kane! Of course, Harry Kane will never have to make cold calls for a living. But even in the mid-1980s, the man on the end of the line thought it was a prank call. He only had my word for it that I was Geoff Hurst, and couldn't believe that England's hattrick hero was trying to flog him insurance over the phone.

It wasn't always so different when I had started working for real. One day I walked into a motor dealership. I approached the desk and, presenting my card to the woman behind it, asked to see the boss. She got up and disappeared into the office at the back. A few moments later this man emerged. He walked over, looked me in the eye and casually flicked my card onto the desk. His aim was poor, perhaps deliberately so, and the card with my name on it bounced onto the floor.

'I don't deal with ex-footballers,' he said.

This man easily could have stayed hidden in his office and sent my card back with a polite but firm no from his secretary. Instead, he chose to get up and come out, and make sure it was me before he insulted me and my profession.

Just another day in the afterlife of a World Cup winner.

Eventually the state started to pay tribute. Alf, with his knighthood, and Mooro with an OBE, were honoured straight away. I never told him this but I didn't necessarily agree with the idea of picking out one member of the team and not honouring the others. The team is the team. But there was nothing I could do about it and eventually they started dishing out awards to some of us. Bobby Charlton was given an OBE in 1969, a CBE in 1974 after he retired and a knighthood in 1994. Banksy heard he'd won an OBE the day before he produced his famous save against Brazil in 1970. Jack was made an OBE in 1974. An MBE came my way in 1977, and a knighthood in 1998.

I thought the knighthood was a wind-up, and I didn't initially believe it. It's customary to keep quiet about these things before they're announced and I truly believed that it wasn't a scam only when the press started to call me for my reaction about a month later. One of the reasons it just seemed unlikely was the lack of any form of honour for five of my teammates. My knighthood was never talked about, and none of them teased me about it, or displayed any sign of resentment, but the anomaly may well have rankled. The British people sometimes make their own awards, of course, which is why Mooro is always thought of as Sir Bobby and on Merseyside my old strike partner was long known as Sir Roger. But a campaign eventually righted the wrong and in 2000 Roger, George, Ray, Bally and Nobby were awarded long-overdue MBEs. They made their way to Buckingham Palace in lounge suits, having decided beforehand against morning suits because, according to Bally, Nobby's tails would have dragged along the ground. A bit rich coming from someone who was also five foot six!

I suppose my knighthood helped oil the wheels of diplomacy when Sir Bobby Charlton and I were both enlisted to support the FA's bid to get the World Cup back to England in 2006. Finally, the FA had found a proper use for two of its World Cup winners. Having a pair of knights spearhead the challenge presumably looked good on the letterhead. I did it because it felt like a prestigious thing to be involved in. The role called for an awful lot of flying all over the world to persuade FIFA delegates to take our bid seriously. At a certain point, they all made their way to the UK, which is how I found myself making a speech of welcome to the execs at the Natural History Museum. This was daunting enough. But to ensure the Francophone delegates didn't feel left out, part of the speech had to be in French. I've got four O levels: in technical drawing, metalwork, maths and science. If you ask which was most useful to me, I'd say maths, for counting how many goals I'd scored. None, you'll notice, was in French. But the job was to do what you're told. So the FA assigned a great teacher to me by the name of Jane Bateman, and she coaxed me towards competence. Blimey, doing that speech was worth a knighthood on its own.

During the two or three years of schmoozing FIFA delegates to look on our bid with favour, I came to understand that our efforts were doomed to failure. The sports minister Tony Banks was involved, and he roped in the PM, Tony Blair. We strategised at the highest level. And yet it felt like the whole process was an absolute waste of time. Us showing them the grounds, them smiling and having their pictures taken with us, it was no more than a charade, a performance.

At a certain point, I started to wonder if the bidding process may actually be corrupt. This was before the investigations by the *Sunday Times*, the exposé by *Panorama* or, more recently, the four-part Netflix *FIFA Uncovered* laid out quite how rotten an institution football's world governing body was. The greater scandals were still to come. In one notorious voting session, FIFA allocated the World Cup to Russia in 2018, when England would be mysteriously humiliated in the voting process, and Qatar in 2022. FIFA was later cleared of corruption in the voting, but the conduct exposed was shocking.

Even in the late 1990s, if you dealt with these preening delegates, you just knew. All the faffing about we did to convince people that England would be a suitable host seemed to bear no relevance to the decision. We were one of the top football nations and they were fully aware of the facilities we had to offer. Entertaining them as we did, it was really about softening them up. They got a nice holiday in London out of it and wasted everybody's time. Once, I remember, we were entertaining senior FIFA delegates from countries I won't name. We hosted them at a formal dinner with an absolute tableful of bigwigs and my old pal Martin Peters. I see from the table plan I still have that I sat next to Alan Sugar and Sir Bobby was placed next to Ms Diane Abbott. One of the FIFA delegates turned up drunk an hour late. That illustrates precisely how much respect such delegates had for the process. At another dinner we attended, one of the delegates actually fell asleep at the table.

Above all, there was the reverence for Sepp Blatter, the president of FIFA. It made Judith and me feel uncomfortable. We witnessed his arrival at a FIFA function somewhere in the world. The deafening applause that greeted his entrance left a sour taste in the mouth. In the end, I just wanted to ask the top brass at the FA and in government why they were wasting their time dealing with such a seemingly bent organisation. But my job was to be a good sport.

Of course, the footballer who had the greatest second act of us all was the one who managed to steer clear of any entanglement with football institutions. Jimmy Greaves always had the natural wit and instinctive timing of a stand-up comedian. Once he'd successfully managed to overcome his addiction to alcohol, he was destined to become a great entertainer. So it proved. Every Saturday lunchtime, he twinkled on the nation's TV screens in tandem with Roger's old Liverpool striking partner Ian St John. Jimmy seemed to have rebranded his image. He was now known as Greavsie, and he grew a moustache that was splayed like a ferret across that moon face of his. But live in the studio there was no disguising the sharpness and speed of thought that marked him out as England's deadliest marksman.

So Jimmy had the last laugh. He even won a World Cup medal in the end. This came about as the result of a change of heart by FIFA. Until 1978, it awarded winners' and losers' medals only to those who'd played in the World Cup final. In 2007 they decided to award retrospective medals to all squad members, and the coaching staff too. At a reception in 10 Downing Street in 2009, the 1966 squad received theirs from the prime minister, Gordon Brown. George Cohen went along to accept Alf's belated medal on behalf of Lady Ramsey.

The day of the ceremony was timed to coincide with a home game for England. That evening the medallists all paraded onto the pitch at Wembley before a qualifier against Andorra. In a lively little cameo on TV, Jimmy gave his scathing verdict on the quality of the opposition, suggesting that even the old men who'd earlier been presented with their medals could hold their own against the Pyrenean visitors. According to his son Andy, they couldn't get him off the screen fast enough.

Five years later he sold his medal at auction. Then in 2015 he had a debilitating stroke and his family found themselves without the funds to pay for his treatment. Terry Baker, his agent and mine, raised over £150,000, while the FA made what they called a discretionary donation. Finally, in the depths of the pandemic in 2020 and nine months before his death, at the age of 80 Jimmy Greaves was made an MBE. It was the very least he deserved.

9

THE
BROTHERS

B obby and Jack. Jack and Bobby. We all felt it was fantastic to have two brothers in the team. To this day, I still think it's quite remarkable that the Charltons performed together at the very highest level.

There have been other brothers who have played together in World Cups. Let's just take the European nations where a lot of them, weirdly, have been Dutch: the Van der Kerkhof twins, the Koemans, the De Boer twins. For Denmark there were the Laudrups. Two Försters played for West Germany. I'd love to be able to say the Charltons are the only brothers to win the World Cup together, but that's not quite true. If you root around the competition's archives, up pop Fritz and Ottmar Walter of West Germany who beat the great Magyars of Puskás and Hidegkuti in 1954.

But in my era there was only one set of brothers that anyone talked about. And since then, no surname in English football has ever resonated quite as much. Not Matthews or Finney, Lineker or Gascoigne. By the time David Beckham was captain of England, it was far easier for his fame to spread around the world. The name of Charlton was known every-where on footballing merit alone. It used to be said you could walk into a bar in the most politically hostile country in the world and the mention of Bobby Charlton would bring smiles to stony faces.

I loved them both. That said, you could not possibly get two brothers who were more different. And this was absolutely apparent on the pitch as much as off it. If Bobby played like an aristocrat, Jack was more of a blue-collar worker. Where Bobby was often painfully shy, Jack was a social animal. Bobby was a great ambassador for club and country who could be relied upon to conduct himself immaculately. Jack liked a fag and a pint and a laugh, and fitted right in when he went off to manage the Republic of Ireland. It's a measure of the distance between them as footballers that Bobby won his first cap for England when he was just 20, whereas Jack was nearly 30.

Bobby's natural soulmate in the team was Ray Wilson. They roomed together and seemed to fit like a glove. I can't remember who Jack roomed with but whoever it was they would have had to put up with his messiness and his taste for an argument. He was a wonderful character, but he was always taking issue with people about something or other – though even he came to realise that there was no point in trying to win an argument with Alf Ramsey. 'Alf, you're talking shit,' he once said to him. 'That's as it may be, Jack, but of course you will do as I ask.' Bobby, on the other hand, was so averse to conflict he was booked only twice in over 750 games. Or roughly once every decade. The first time his name went in the book was in the quarter-final against Argentina. In the confusion he had no idea it had happened. This was before the invention of yellow cards, which signalled the caution to both the player and the crowd. In the melee after the game no one got round to telling Bobby and he only found out about it three decades later when it came up in conversation with someone from FIFA. He picked up the booking for arguing with the referee, but what's worth remembering is that he was coming to his brother's defence. At one point, Jack was muscled to the floor and a gang of Argentine players stood over him threateningly as if about to administer a backstreet kicking. This was what prompted Bobby to get into a spat with the ref. Jack was booked too.

I knew how unlike each other they were as players long before I came to know them as teammates. When West Ham played Manchester United, Bobby would glide around the pitch as if on casters, twisting left or right with grace and subtle power. With his balance and agility he was almost impossible to tackle. He rarely put himself in a position where anybody *could* tackle him. You rarely knew what he was going to do next, and even if you did there wasn't much you could do about it. He could dribble, he could run, he was strong enough to hold off markers and once he got anywhere near the box he could fire off those unstoppable cannonballs with either foot. The famous thunderbolt against Mexico in 1966, England's first goal of the tournament, was the shot that shook the world. Every time you look at it, it's hard to take in quite how fast the ball is travelling.

Bobby scored 49 times for England at not far off a goal every other game. Only three of those goals were penalties. Harry Kane, the current record holder, has scored a third of all his international goals from the spot. Bobby's is an incredible record, a phenomenal strike rate. And he wasn't even a forward!

The only thing Bobby wasn't great at was the physical side. You wouldn't necessarily rely on him in a defensive wall. 'Our kid loves to whack the ball,' Jack once said, 'but he's not so keen to have it whacked at him.' And he wasn't a big tackler. That was Jack's speciality. 'I'm a destroyer, a fouler, a batterer,' Jack said with the smile of a shark when he was a guest on *Parkinson*. I had the chance to see for myself whenever we played Leeds. His legs seemed to go on forever, which gave him considerable reach when he was sliding in to dispossess you. Then there was that long neck of his, which looked as if it had a couple of extra vertebrae. There's a lovely cartoon of Jack in *Goal* magazine in the 1960s where he mostly consists of neck. It made him incredibly hard to beat in the air.

He and Norman Hunter, who would also be selected for the 1966 squad, were a formidable partnership at the back for Leeds. They were two of the toughest defenders around. Norman was a lovely guy but totally brutal. When he made his international debut in the famous wingless 2–0 victory in Madrid in December 1965, it was as England's first official substitute. As he trotted onto the pitch, Alan Ball put his hands together in prayer and said, 'For what they are about to receive.' It's no accident that he was known by the least subtle nickname in football: Norman 'Bites Yer Legs' Hunter. I don't remember that he, or Jack, ever bit mine too hard, because I seemed to come off the field without any bruises. Maybe they liked me?

Jack used to pretend that he wasn't interested in the beauty of the game. 'I've always had a distrust of centre backs who can play,' he once said. 'I like centre backs who stop other people playing.' That's why Alf selected him. 'I have a pattern of players in my mind,' he famously told Jack, 'and I pick the best players to fit the pattern.' Jack wasn't necessarily the best stopper in England, but he was right for Alf. That must be why Alf was happy to let Brian Labone, who'd been an England regular and took part in the pre-tournament training at Lilleshall, have the summer off to get married. He didn't need him. I don't think Alf's frankness would have bothered Jack too much. He wasn't at all precious. He knew what he was best at was stopping players playing. Alf agreed. 'I know you won't trust Bobby Moore,' Alf added. What he meant was Jack was Mooro's insurance policy. There they stood, side by side at the heart of England's back four, but when it entered the captain's head to do something creative further upfield, Jack could be depended upon to stay behind and mind the shop. Plus he was a bit quicker than Mooro.

Not that Jack didn't drift upfield himself now and then. Watch the World Cup final again and you'll see him pop up all over the pitch. On either wing, in the German box. It easily could have been him who made it to 2–1, because he was standing right next door to Martin Peters. He might have joked that he'd have cleared the bar but Jack scored six goals for England, and not all were with his head. There was more to his game than people recognise.

So Jack and Bobby may not have had much in common, as brothers, as players, as characters, but as far as Alf was concerned, they were both indispensable. Was there something in the water of Ashington? Or was football in the brothers' blood?

I never went to Ashington, and I only ever met their mother Cissie once, on the day England won the World Cup and we all celebrated at the Royal Garden Hotel. West Ham may have provided three of the team's winners. Cissie had produced two on her own! No wonder she had her picture taken that night with the prime minister, Harold Wilson, who flew back from America to be at Wembley. More likely, he had his picture taken with Cissie. She must have been a powerful driving force.

The drive seems to have been to get her sons a better life. All of my teammates came from working-class roots. Bob Moore lagged pipes in a power station. Harry Cohen was a gas fitter. William Peters was a Thames lighterman, James Greaves a tube driver. And these are just the Londoners. If life could be tough in the south, it was a harder graft in the northeast. For every day of his working life Bob Charlton went far underground to mine coal. It was a dirty and life-threatening job but in Ashington there were few other opportunities for work.

For a while, it looked as if that's where Jack would end up. But he did one shift down the pit as a teenager, came back up into the open air and resigned from his apprenticeship straight off. That says something about his personality. He always did know what he wanted, and must have seen at once that he wasn't suited to a life underground. He was too much in love with the open air.

The alternative to the pit was the pitch. Cissie's family was full of naturally talented sportsmen. The most successful of them was her cousin Jackie Milburn, who played in three FA Cup finals for Newcastle in the 1950s. For nearly 50 years until Alan Shearer came along, he was the club's record goal-scorer. He played for England too. To see him in action, Jack and Bobby had to go to a local fleapit.

The really fundamental difference between the brothers was there at the start. It may have been a good way out, but

Jack wasn't that into football as a kid. He didn't play his first school game till he was in his teens. It seems as if it was almost a surprise to him when Leeds took him on at 17. Bobby, on the other hand, was so good at football that from an early age there was no question he'd ever do anything else. He was 15 when he first caught the eye of Matt Busby when playing for England Schoolboys, and he was soon apprenticed to Manchester United.

If you look at the names they rubbed shoulders with in those early years, it's as if their football roots belong in a bygone era. When Bobby first played for England his captain was Billy Wright, who was first capped the year after the war. An early manager of Jack's was Raich Carter, who made his name scoring hatfuls for Sunderland in the 1930s.

Then came Munich. The runway plane crash on 6 February 1958 killed eight of the so-called Busby Babes and claimed 23 lives in all. It was first and foremost a calamity for Manchester United. The lasting shockwaves it sent through English football were similar to those felt at the tragedy of Hillsborough in 1989. Football was never quite the same again. Symbolically it divided the football of yesteryear from the modern era.

The impact on Bobby was incalculable. It's hard enough for me now to deal with the loss of teammates I've known for 60 years. But to play with those boys one day and then lose eight of them in one random tragedy – it's impossible even to imagine how Bobby coped with the massive burden over those years. The greatest loss of all was the death aged 21 of Duncan Edwards, who lasted in hospital for two weeks after the crash. Bobby would have expected to play alongside him for years to come, for Manchester United and for England.

This may seem strange – or it may not – but the Munich air crash was never mentioned between us. Not when Bobby was at the peak of his powers and he represented the hopes of club and country. Nor when I came to know him much better as the elder statesman of English football. I certainly wouldn't have brought it up because to go there would have felt too intrusive. In fact, I didn't realise until much more recently that Bobby only knew the plane had crashed when he emerged from unconsciousness, still strapped in his seat, which had been flung from the wreckage.

What everyone who knew him seemed to agree was that he boarded the plane as a carefree kid. He came round older and sadder, with the hopes of English football heaped on his shoulders. Already a bit introverted, he now became even more so. And the difference between the brothers only widened. Basically Jack was open, Bobby was closed. Jack affectionately called his brother 'our Robert' or 'our kid'. Bobby referred to Jack as 'Jack'. What you saw with Jack was what you got. I'd love to have been a fly on the wall when he was first told by his manager Don Revie that he'd been called up for the England squad in April 1965. He learned just after Leeds had beaten Manchester United in a semi-final replay of the FA Cup with a late goal. Straight after the game an ecstatic Jack barged into the Man U dressing to break the good news to Bobby. It must have been like walking into a funeral parlour wearing a party hat. Bobby quietly congratulated him. 'I'm pleased for you,' he said. Another Man U player told Jack to fuck off. Later, he would concede that his excitement was a bit tin-eared.

I first played with both of them when I made my debut for England against West Germany on 23 February 1966. It wasn't a great game for me. One reporter said I looked lost. I played in four more away games before the World Cup started, and Bobby was rested for the last of them. So by the time I was drafted back into the side for the quarter-final against Argentina, I'd had relatively little exposure to his style of play. But I knew that if I could get the ball to him, things would happen. It was easy to click with him because he was such a natural player. He was just an absolute pleasure to play with.

Fast-forward to the World Cup semi-final. England against Portugal. In the build-up one Portuguese player paid Bobby the biggest compliment: 'He is more difficult to mark than Pelé. Pelé goes only one way – forward. Charlton will go back 50 yards to gain two.' That sums him up well. Despite the worry he'd miss the game with a stiff neck, Bobby went on to give one of his greatest performances in an England shirt. 'I felt as though I could run all night that night,' he later said.

After the ugliness of the quarter-final, the semi was a wonderful exhibition of positive, free-flowing football with barely any foul play. We went ahead just after the half-hour thanks to Bobby. Roger Hunt ran on to a lofted long ball from Ray Wilson; the goalkeeper ran out to meet the danger but could only clear to the edge of the box. There Bobby was waiting. Calmly he drilled a grass-cutter first-time into the net.

Charlton 1 Portugal 0.

It was the biggest game I'd ever played in. We were on the brink of an even bigger one, but as the second half progressed we looked for a cushion to make our place in the final safe.

Then in three eventful minutes the Charlton brothers demonstrated more starkly than ever before that they were cut from very different cloth.

In the 79th minute, George Cohen took the ball just inside our half. He dribbled for a bit, looking for options, and spotted me up ahead, so he chipped a pass up to the right-hand corner of the penalty area for me to run on to. I had the Portuguese full back José Carlos to contend with, and it might have looked like more his ball than mine. He may have thought so too, but I was bigger and stronger. In the TV footage it looks as if he went into a revolving door before me and came out after. Facing away from the goal with the ball at my feet, I then looked up to see Bobby dashing towards the box, as I knew he would be. He wasn't quite there yet so I had to hang on for just the right moment to cue him up. Luckily Carlos, who could see I wasn't intending to shoot, seemed caught in two minds and held off. But still the lay-off needed to be perfectly weighted. It must be one of the softest passes I ever made, a gentle golf putt. I rolled it into the path of Bobby at the edge of the box, who 99 times out of 100 you'd expect to score from there. And he did. He absolutely clobbered the ball into the far corner.

Charlton 2 Portugal 0.

We were in the final. Or we hoped we were. Then in the 82nd minute António Simões lifted a cross from the right towards José Torres on the far post. Torres was a bit of a lamppost and Jack had been struggling with him all game. Now he sent a header looping back across the goal. Gordon Banks waved a hand at it but was beaten. Jack, also beaten, then flapped a hand at it too. It was a snap calculation of a professional stopper. If he hadn't handballed, Jack knew there was no one else to prevent the ball going in. At least with a penalty, there was a chance that Banksy would save it, or Eusébio might miss. He didn't.

Charlton 2 Portugal 1.

We were hanging on then. There was a nerve-shredding wait for the final whistle. We told ourselves not to make mistakes, to keep hold of the ball and waste as much time as we could. I'd been in that situation before, and would be again, but the worry we felt in those last eight minutes was off the chart.

Deliberate handballs were much more common in those days. Now no defender would do what Jack did because it would mean an automatic red card and a one-match ban. So he'd miss the final. When Paul Gascoigne got a second booking in the World Cup semi-final in Turin in 1990, the tears he shed said everything. He knew that he wouldn't be playing if England managed to beat West Germany. At the end of our game, Jack cried too as he hugged Bobby. But they were tears of joy. And possibly of relief. The Charltons were in the final.

Their dad Bob was working underground that day and missed the whole family drama. The National Coal Board ever so graciously gave him time off to watch a repeat.

The Charltons' World Cup story continued in 1970, although Jack was no longer a first choice. Both brothers knew when we left Mexico after losing to West Germany in the quarter-final that they would never play for England again. So while their international careers started far apart, they ended together.

When they finished playing altogether, the differences between them became apparent in other ways. While still a player with Leeds, Jack quietly went about doing his FA coaching badges at Lilleshall alongside men who would go on to become great managers – Bobby Robson, Dave Sexton, Lawrie McMenemy. So when he retired he was ready. He was a natural in that commanding role because he knew what he wanted and never had a problem telling players to do it his way. After all, he never had a problem shouting as a player either. I was never bawled at by him – probably because I was too far away – but Banksy, Nobby and Ray definitely all were. He would concede that one of the biggest influences on his thinking as a coach was Alf. Alf liked structure and method and plans. So did Jack.

I watched his progress with the Republic of Ireland from afar. I'm not going to say I was a huge admirer of his playing philosophy. The idea was to lump the ball up towards the corner flag, chase hard and put the opposition under pressure where they least liked it. The central midfielders who saw the ball flying constantly overhead may as well have been plane-spotting. You'd never have guessed that in all but one of Jack's 35 caps for England he played alongside Bobby Moore. Mooro's cultured influence obviously didn't count for much! But Jack's direct style was effective enough to get a small footballing nation all the way to the Euros in 1988, where he took great pleasure in beating England. Then in the 1990 World Cup in Italy he got them to the quarter-finals, and in the 1994 finals in the USA they managed to beat Italy. I couldn't have been more pleased for him.

Bobby, on the other hand, didn't seem to be cut out for management. Gifted players often find it hard to coach those of more modest ability. He was much more suited to the ambassadorial role of bidding to host the World Cup. Bobby was ideal in that job. It wasn't just that everyone he met got a visible thrill from shaking the hand of a very great player. It was also that he could be guaranteed never to say the wrong thing. He knew the task was to coax and persuade, and not stick his foot in his mouth. Even when it became apparent that nothing we did or said bore any relevance to the decision, Bobby was far too discreet to say anything. Jack would have been nudging me halfway through some big FIFA function and saying exactly what he thought: 'What a fucking waste of time this is!'

It was this quality that made Jack such a brilliant entertainer. He may have been one of the less natural footballers in the team, but he was the most natural after-dinner speaker. He would knock spots off most of the rest of us, including Bobby who was still a very polished and confident speaker. Only Jimmy Greaves could match him as a comic wit, although Bally, who'd introduced himself as 'your after-dinner squeaker', was a gifted performer too. Jack would stand up and I'd see him extract from his pocket a piece of paper that he'd had for so long it mainly seemed to consist of creases. Those were his speech notes, though I'm not convinced he ever needed them.

I don't think it's a coincidence that he was the only one of us to be a castaway on *Desert Island Discs*. He was honest, and open, and he could time a laugh. One signature of his was use of the F word. Bobby rarely swore, if ever. Jack was very comfortable turning the air blue. If he was giving a speech, it always added to the flavour of the story. In fact, he was so forthright it was sometimes more of a shock when he didn't swear. Once, we were driving somewhere on the M1 and we stopped at a service station. Jack was in the middle of his fish and chips when somebody came over wanting a photo of the two of us.

'OK,' said Jack, 'but not till I've finished my fish and chips.' Not an F-word in sight.

While I was working on this book, the spirit of Jack visited me in the strangest of ways. It happened on the day I was dropping my wife off at Heathrow. She was flying out to Chicago to visit her younger sister, who had just been widowed. We were eating in a hotel restaurant at Terminal 5 when a couple who were roughly our age sat down just across from us. I assumed the man recognised me because he tapped me on the shoulder as we were leaving to say hello. He told me he was a retired detective, but in 1966 he'd been a copper on duty on the evening of the World Cup final when he'd bumped into a pissed Jack Charlton in the small hours of the night. And he loaned him a coat. Now, here he was telling me about it, 58 years later. I never found out how or why a bobby would have a spare coat.

At the end of the World Cup, the four semi-finalists all attended the gala dinner that night at the Royal Garden Hotel. So Eusébio, who finished the top scorer with nine goals in the tournament, was there too. In a lovely gesture of friendship and respect, he presented Bobby with a case of port. Somehow that just sums up the Charltons. On the greatest night of their lives, Bobby got a classy gift from one of the world's greatest players, while Jack got a coat from a copper.

I can't reminisce about the two of them without mentioning that over the years the brothers would become distanced from each other. This was maybe a natural result of the difference in their personalities opening up a gulf once they were no longer playing. But there was also a family disagreement that reportedly had to do with Cissie and Bobby's wife Norma. It was characteristic of Jack to be more open about it than Bobby, sometimes inappropriately so. I'm not going to claim I have any extra light to shed on these private relationships. It just wasn't the sort of thing we talked about when we got together. Each brother must have understood that I was equally fond of them, as we all were, and Judith and I always found both Norma and Jack's wife Pat to be very friendly. What I do know is that in the many times I saw the brothers together across the decades, there was very little sign that the two of them struggled to get on.

And the mutual respect was obviously there. I saw it for myself from feet away on the night in December 2008 when Bobby was presented with the BBC Sports Personality of the Year Lifetime Achievement Award. Bobby was in the audience next to Norma while many of his old teammates from Man United and England – among them George and Ray, Roger and a beaming Nobby – were waiting to greet him. Bobby came up onstage to a standing ovation that lasted for a minute and a half. He looked genuinely overcome by the love and respect in the room. Then, after an introduction from Gary Lineker, on loped Jack wearing a big grin. Right in front of me, they shook hands, and then they hugged, and Jack gave him the award. No one stood closer to them at that moment than I did, and to me the expression of love between them, though perhaps a little awkward with so many people watching, looked spontaneous and genuine. As the clapping stopped and silence fell, Jack spoke with feeling.

'He's Wor Bob. He's always been Wor Bob. He's always been me younger brother. When we were kids and we used to go to the park and play, I would go home for dinner and he'd stay on all day. He's loved his football and he's never put it at risk in any way, shape or form. Bobby Charlton is the greatest player I've ever seen. He's my brother.'

As the audience applauded this tribute, Jack leaned in to Bobby and spoke into his ear.

'Well done, kid.'

Jack and Bobby. Bobby and Jack. Our brothers.

10

JUDITH AND THE WAGS

B obby and Norma: 63 years. Jack and Pat, Gordon and Ursula, Ray and Pat: 62. George and Daphne: 60. Martin and Kathy: 55. Nobby and Kay: 49. Alan and Lesley: 37. Most of the marriages of the 1966 team were solid and durable. Only Mooro and Roger went through divorces and married again. Only Jimmy did things his way: he and Irene married in their teens, divorced in the depths of his alcoholism but couldn't bear to be apart and went on to spend 63 years together.

Marriages started earlier in those days. So that's one reason why they could last so long. According to my own wife – and I'm quoting her here – perhaps they endured because this was also a time when women 'weren't as bothered about having big careers and were content with being housewives and mums'. But does that list of long, successful marriages also say something about Alf's nose for a certain type of personality? He always liked footballers who could be depended upon, team players rather than show ponies and Jack the Lads, and maybe that showed in the way we lived our lives too.

The publication of this book happens to coincide with the 60th anniversary of Judith's and my wedding. It's been a wonderful marriage that has made my life rich in everything I could wish for. Yes, we have suffered a tragedy too with the death of our oldest daughter, Claire. But where some marriages cannot take the strain of such loss, we have always known how to rely on each other. Our commitment, mine to her and hers to me, has never wavered. 'You either grow together or you grow apart,' says Judith. We grew together.

So I want to spend this chapter talking about Judith and exploring – with a lot of input from her – what it was like to be married to a famous footballer in the 1960s.

As my teammates also discovered, it was a good time to come from humble beginnings. This was the decade when things changed for people from a working-class background. There was a bit less deference around than there had been in the 1950s. You were no longer expected to know your place. Unlike Alf, who was a generation older than us, we didn't have to change how we spoke in order to fit in. And for people like Judith, there were the first green shoots of media interest in the wives of footballers.

At West Ham, there was a little flurry of it before the FA Cup final in 1964 when the newspapers spotted that a lot of us were soon to tie the knot. 'Four players are due to sign wedding forms this year,' one of them reported. Another sports section did a photo feature on the four Hammers and their brides-to-be. Snaps were taken in the players' room at Upton Park, and then out on the pitch. There's a picture of my fiancée kicking a ball in her high heels. 'Judith, a nurse at a children's nursery, lives at East Ham,' it said. 'She met Geoff Hurst four years ago at a dance. They'll spend their honeymoon at their new home in Hornchurch.'

We actually first knew each other when still at school. She always says she thought I was a big 'ead. I was tall and girls did seem to like me, so perhaps I was! She was small – she still stands at five foot not much – but hers was a big presence. She was full of life and attitude. We'd hang around at the same youth centre and then went to dances above the Chelmsford Odeon. We had the same bus route home. One night, when it was time to leave, she was getting irritated by the fact that I wasn't showing signs of commitment and stomped off to catch a different bus that went to her house but not mine. When she came down from the top deck at her stop, she found me waiting for her on the lower deck.

'What are you doing?' she said.

'Taking you home.'

We've been together ever since.

It turned out I already knew her father Jack Harries because he played cricket for Chelmsford. Not long ago, I came across a team photo of him sitting next to me, a teenage batsman with no thought in his head that this good medium-pace bowler with a moustache and a dry sense of humour was my future father-in-law. Judith did her best with my parents. My father Charlie was more of a pushover. He didn't have a nasty bone in his body, although he could be unpredictable, bringing home random people after a night bashing out songs at the piano in the pub. My mother Evelyn found it harder to accept Judith. She got the sense that her future mother-in-law thought I could have married the daughter of a doctor or a solicitor. It took many years for my mother to admit she'd been wrong about my wife.

Judith and the other wives and girlfriends were back in front of the camera after West Ham won the FA Cup and shared the Charity Shield. The players posed in kit with the trophies and the club thought it would be fun to do a photoshoot of their other halves in the players' room at Upton Park. I sat second from the right in my team photo, and so did Judith in hers. Tina Moore, the closest we then had to a celebrity wife, stood where Mooro always did, in the back row on the right, her arms folded in the pose of a proper footballer.

The photo suggests that the club looked after the wives of the players. Up to a point, that's true. Before we had our own training ground we would train all over east London. For a while, we went to a fantastic pitch in Tilbury, right next door to the Bata shoe factory. One day the club invited the wives and girlfriends along to select a free pair of shoes. 'They definitely weren't designer,' Judith remembers. Such were the perks of being in a relationship with a footballer in the early 1960s.

The club splashed out more generously in the summer of 1963. When West Ham got to the final of the American International Soccer League in the US, they decided to fly our wives and girlfriends over to New York for a fortnight. This was possibly a way of saying sorry for having dragged us away for much of the summer. Half of them had never flown or been abroad before, so it was an adventure. By way of preparation, Judith bought her first bikini in a shop in Romford and was appalled at the price: three quid! Few of us were married then so the ladies were accommodated separately, but there was a certain amount of room swapping and the club trainer in charge turned a blind eye.

Otherwise the wives didn't see much of us and had to explore the city under their own steam. Judith and Kathy Peters discovered an eye-popping new world on the New York subway.

For some of us, there was one memorable night out at the Copacabana where Al Martino was performing. You have to be quite old to recall his songs but in 1952 the Italian-American crooner had the first ever UK number one with 'Here in My Heart'. He is better remembered for playing Johnny Fontane, the singer connected to the mob in *The Godfather*. Remember the horse's head I mentioned in 'Meeting Alf'? That scene happens thanks to Al Martino's character. When a Hollywood producer refuses to give him a role in a film, he wakes up next to the severed head of his favourite stallion. Anyway, it was a thrilling evening.

Meanwhile, back at Upton Park, Judith came to all the home games, and her dad came with her. Her main memory is that they were hosted in a tearoom with no windows. At half time they would go in to a big pot of tea that was stone cold and a platter of sandwiches that she was convinced had been made a week earlier. The standards of catering suggested that the comfort of the wives was not a priority. Some of them got fed up and one week, having poked their fingers in the sandwiches, they left a note requesting hot tea and fresh sandwiches for the next home game. The tea lady, who was a force to be reckoned with, went straight to the board and complained at this outrage. I would have been oblivious to all this until Ron Greenwood instructed me to ask Judith to apologise. She must have been identified as the shop steward in all this. Initially she refused but eventually gave in, said sorry and conceded that the request could have been made differently. The tea lady still blew her top at her.

Judith made her feelings known as a spectator too. An old cutting from one of the scrapbooks is a ghostwritten column by me in the *People*. I describe how in the early days whenever I wasn't playing well she had no qualms about shouting down fans who were giving me a hard time. 'My wife Judith turned on the taunters one day in the stand. "The next one of you who says anything against my Geoff will get a swipe with this" … and she picked up her umbrella menacingly.' Judith now says this is wrong on two counts. One, she'd never say 'my Geoff', and, two, she wouldn't take a brolly to the games. Although it was always done in fun, what actually happened was she flicked peanuts at my critics. 'If I'd had a brick,' she adds, 'it would have been a brick.'

Another time she got into trouble when parking our car at the ground. Normally we drove together to home games but on this occasion I must have gone in ahead and she arrived alone. As she queued to get in she saw the attendant taking money from the driver in front. This wasn't a paying car park so he was accepting a bung. When her turn came to enter, this attendant refused to let her in even though he knew she was my wife. She drove in anyway as he held on to her car door. She can still picture the man's face today. 'He said he was going to report me because my name wasn't on the list. I said, "Funnily enough, I'm going to do the same to you." I didn't because he got to the board first.' Ron then came to me and asked me to make sure Judith had her name down for the car park. 'It's embarrassing to have her arguing,' he said with a sigh.

Ron actually liked Judith, and they got on well. In his description, she was the perfect footballer's wife. What he probably meant was that she accepted the status quo of a life ruled by the game's strict schedules. Ron felt some wives could be too

influential over their husbands, and too distracting. He didn't
want wives to interfere – he even told her so. She may have
grumbled in private, but she was just very supportive.

To buy our first house after we got married, Judith and
I had to sell our Ford Anglia. It was my first car – I got it for
460 quid on the Southend arterial road and used it to get to
training. Now, I went by rail; a centre forward in our youth team
called Mike Beesley picked me up from Romford station in his
Renault Dauphine and, quite rightly, charged me petrol money.
In Hornchurch, we lived in a tight little community of footballers. While the Peters family were next door, other West Ham
couples were round the corner on the same estate.

In the early days, whenever we first socialised outside that
group we struggled to find out feet. Having both grown up in
Chelmsford we'd barely been anywhere and felt like country
hicks when going out with the older and more socially confident
players. Judith's toes still curl at the memory of the evening out
we had one Christmas in Ilford when she wore an old bridesmaid's dress and nervously spilled her dinner down the front.

Later, we moved to a bigger house in Chigwell. In order
to afford it we sold not only our old home but every stick of
furniture in it. Our housewarming was a bring-your-own-chair
party. Something changed for us when we made that move. It
was our first big house and Judith said she felt a coolness from
some other wives at West Ham. Maybe they thought that, with
the vice-chairman living in the same road, we were suddenly
looking down on them. No such idea ever entered our heads,
but she found it very difficult. 'I'm a girl from a council house
in Chelmsford,' she still says to this day. Her sense was that they

thought she'd changed, whereas it was their attitude to her that seemed different. My attitude was to ignore it. One night we were going out to a function and she was very worried about wearing her mink short jacket because it would trigger gossip among other wives. 'Let them all talk about you,' I said. 'You haven't done anything.'

It was destabilising not to know whose friendship she could trust in. We had one neighbour who didn't drive and was struggling with her children, so in the goodness of her heart Judith decided to be helpful and chauffeur her around. Then one day she'd just dropped her off somewhere when she overheard this woman explaining, 'I've no worries getting here. Geoff Hurst's wife drives me.' That was the last taxi ride. There was another time when the wife of a business friend of mine was in a local hospital. They didn't live nearby so Judith kindly offered to put this man up for the night. I wasn't there that evening – we must have had an away game – but Tina Moore was. Perhaps because Tina had experience of this too, she asked this man if he was friends with us because we were Judith and Geoff or because our names were Judith and Geoff Hurst. Did he like us for ourselves, in other words, or because I was a successful footballer? 'I can't honestly answer that,' he replied as he drank our wine. Judith found this so deeply insulting that she asked him to leave. When he just sat there she went off to bed in a steaming rage and ordered Tina to get him out of the house. 'I don't care how,' she said. 'Get him out.'

If Judith got on with Ron, it was quite a different story with Alf. Alf ran the England camp like a monastery. He sealed us off from the rest of our lives, so marital contact was restricted to talking on the phone. One evening after one of the group games in the World Cup, as a concession the wives were all allowed back to Hendon Hall Hotel. Alf must have conceded that this would be good for squad morale. But Judith had only just arrived with Tina and they were in the bar when Alf came in and announced to the room, 'Goodnight, ladies. Goodnight, gentleman.' Mooro had the pluck to object that he'd only just got us a drink. And Alf simply repeated himself. 'Goodnight, ladies. Goodnight, gentlemen.' And that was it. When Alf says 'go' you go. Although I'd been part of the set-up for only six months, Judith was already aware of how the regime was run. With the other wives, she got up, got her coat and went home.

In my seven years as an England international, Judith had precisely three conversations with Alf. All were brief. The first was in the tunnel under the stands at Wembley after we'd won the World Cup. The wives were going round to the rendezvous point where they'd meet the players when she bumped into Alf. 'Congratulations,' she said. 'It's not me,' he said. 'I didn't win it.' Part of the story of that day is Alf's refusal to take part in public displays of euphoria. Judith found that it was the same in private too.

Her memory of the rest of the day is a bit blurred, and overlaid by the television images. The night before, Judith was one of seven women staying at the Royal Garden Hotel who went out to *The Black and White Minstrel Show*. So, although she can't remember how it happened, there must have been some attempt by someone at the FA to organise an entertainment for them. Also in the press photo are Alan Ball's fiancée Lesley, Kay Stiles, Norma Charlton, Pat Wilson, Carol Paine and Ursula Banks. Judith was caught in one snap with a down-turned mouth. 'I look really thrilled to be there,' she tells me. The next day they made their way to Wembley, Judith accompanied as ever by her dad. To get hold of their tickets, she had to walk round the lower ground floor corridor of the stadium to a big doorway where she and other wives would wait outside it until we came out and handed the tickets over. Touts would hang around there like vultures.

Later, as the teams lined up on the pitch for the anthems, Mooro would give a coded signal to Tina, clasping his hands above his head. Judith knew I was far too single-minded for such romantic gestures. 'There wasn't a cat in hell's chance you were going to give me a wave,' she says. 'You wouldn't know if I was standing on the roof!' I suspect she's probably right. For the record, the seats weren't on the roof, they were reasonably low down, on the opposite side of the pitch from the cameras, so Judith experienced my three goals from the other direction. One striking memory she has is of the non-playing squad members, who were sitting in the same block, leaving before the 90 minutes were up so they could be pitchside at the final whistle. They thought it was all over. The lift went so slowly they missed the German equaliser. Judith recalls that Lesley cried when the ball went in. The squad didn't bother coming back to their seats but watched extra time sitting on the floor by the bench. That must be how Jimmy Greaves ended up sitting on the bench next to Alf and his staff. When I shot against the underside of the crossbar, Judith had no more idea than I did if it had gone over the line, and like me – like all of us – she held her breath. As for the final goal that settled it, the split second that changed my life changed hers too. It put a label on me that both of us have had to live with ever since.

Not that we thought about that then. The wives made their way back to the Royal Garden Hotel. Much has been made of the fact that they were forced to dine separately in a room on a lower floor and watch the endless speeches on a closed-circuit feed. Some may have been upset by the implication that they were somehow not important, but Judith insists that it didn't bother her. She had no desire to sit through a banquet with hundreds of FA and FIFA officials. She enjoyed herself with Tina and Kathy and other wives, many of whom she was sitting down with for the first time. Only years later would she come to know them well. The ones who are still with us are now widows in their eighties and they're all still on our Christmas card list.

The following morning, after a brilliant night out at Danny La Rue's club with Nobby and Kay, Alan and Lesley, and John Connelly and his wife Sandra, there was a breakfast photo call. Judith and I were snapped reading the papers over morning coffee, then we walked hand in hand in Kensington Gardens for another photo. A few weeks later, we went back into town as guests of the *News of the World*, who invited Tom Finney to present me with my man-of-the-match trophy. My favourite photograph from that day is of me driving away in our Austin Morris 1100 with Judith in the passenger seat cradling the cup. Let's face it, in our marriage she's always been the one who handles the crockery!

Judith's second exchange with Alf came four years later. We were in a hotel somewhere. 'I hear you're going to Mexico,' Alf said. 'We're going to bring the pot back.' On reflection, it was less a conversation than another of Alf's prophecies. Judith did indeed go to Mexico in 1970. It came about when a London travel agent invited me, Mooro, Martin and Peter Bonetti to make some personal appearances in order to promote the company. I can't remember if payment was involved, but our wives got an all-expenses-paid trip to the World Cup. There was a press story about them going and Judith remembers with amusement how the photographer was focused on Tina and Peter's first wife Frances, the two glamorous blondes, pushing her and Kathy so far to the back of the shot that they'd soon have ended up behind the sofa.

The four of them were booked into the same hotel as Lady Ramsey but being Alf's wife she kept herself so apart that they never actually spotted her. I didn't see much of Judith either. A couple of times, Alf did permit a visit, but as in 1966 it was strictly curtailed and the physio Harold Shepherdson was as usual clocking the players in and out of the lift. Once, we were in this high-rise hotel in Guadalajara and I was so desperate for fresh air that I nipped out to see Judith on the quiet. We were walking along when I spotted the trainer Les Cocker across the street and without a word dived into a shop as if losing my marker. Another time, Alf allowed me to walk Judith back to her hotel so long as I was back by 12 o'clock. 'You do know what 12 o'clock is, don't you?' he said to me, almost pretending she wasn't there. 'Yes,' she butted in. 'When both hands are pointing upwards!' So ended the third and last exchange between Judith and Alf.

They did cross paths once more. This was in Valletta in 1971. Judith and Kathy liked flying to internationals abroad under their own steam if the location was worth a visit. They knew they'd have no access to their husbands but enjoyed the travel and supporting us. For our Euros qualifying game away to Malta, their travel agent inadvertently booked them into the same hotel as the squad. Knowing this was a big no-no for Alf, they recognised it could lead to embarrassment and had the sense to go virtually into hiding. But they couldn't not eat and eventually Alf spotted them skulking around. At the end of the trip, Alf asked for a quiet word with the husbands of the two miscreant wives. By now Martin and I were two of his most senior players. That didn't stop him threatening us that if Judith or Kathy ever stayed in the team hotel again, we could kiss goodbye to our international careers.

Those trips stopped after I made my last appearance for England the following year. The much bigger change for Judith came when my career was drawing to a close and we started wondering where the money was going to come from next. This was the mid-1970s when even the biggest names in football could never hope to make enough from playing to retire on. So we did what a lot of ex-pros did then. We bought ourselves a pub. Ours was in a quiet village on the edge of Stoke, where we'd moved in 1972. I was briefly at West Brom and then became player-manager of Telford United, and then I was invited by Ron Greenwood to join the coaching staff with England. So for five years, while also giving birth to our third daughter Charlotte in 1977, Judith pulled many more pints than me. By this time, her mother had died, so her father moved in opposite and gave us a lot of help behind the bar. It was a country pub and the customers were mostly regulars.

The pace wasn't hectic, but it wasn't a life she had particularly chosen and when I got a job with Chelsea in 1979, she was very happy to move back south. She was also happy to follow me out to Kuwait for two years, bringing our three daughters with her.

By the time I finished in football for good in 1984, we had been married for 20 years and I think it's safe to say Judith's experience had almost nothing in common with the glamorous life of a modern footballer's wife. In my view, she has been a pioneer as well as a pillar of strength. She threw herself into the role happily and without complaint, but at the same time she has never allowed our family life to be coloured by my celebrity. We have both kept the doors shut on all that, guided by Judith's core belief that in privacy there is dignity.

It's a very long way from Alf to Sven. In Baden-Baden, at the World Cup that England didn't after all get to host in 2006, came the dawn of the wags era. Sven-Göran Eriksson, with his colourful romantic life, was hardly in a position to discourage wives and girlfriends from tagging along, dressing up and colonising the tabloids. Judith quietly rolls her eyeballs at what could be seen as the Beckhamisation of football: the wives' clamouring to be stars in their own right, the players dragging half-a-dozen toddlers in kits onto the pitch after big games. Don't get her started on the libel case unsuccessfully brought by Rebekah Vardy against Coleen Rooney. She firmly believes that the circus has got out of hand.

We both mourn the breakdown in trust between the players and the press. In our day, the hunger for gossip was less ravenous and we felt quite protected by London-based reporters we knew well and even socialised with, like Michael Hart, Brian

James and Reg Drury. They would never have taken advantage of us for a story. One London photographer called Monte Fresco, who invited us to his kids' bar mitzvahs, once playfully addressed Judith as 'Your Ladyshit'.

Monte came along to Buckingham Palace to take the photos when I was knighted in 1998. Technically, from then on, Judith became known as Lady Hurst, but she has always found it extremely uncomfortable whenever anyone addresses her as such. There was a bit of that to contend with whenever she joined me on the World Cup bid trail, often in the company of Bobby and Norma Charlton. We greatly admired both of them and Judith could only marvel at the way Norma knew exactly what was required of the ambassadorial role. I had first-hand experience of this myself once when the bid trail took us to the Bahamas, where there was a big lunchtime meeting. It was extremely hot and I had shorts on. Norma took one look at me and said, 'You're not going lunch like that!' I had to concede she was right. I went straight back to my room and changed into a suit.

Nowadays, my relations with the FA are good and it's become much easier to ask for tickets out of the FA. I take our granddaughter Amy. After a lifetime of being a footballer's wife, Judith decided she'd seen enough games. It's not so much the football that she wants to avoid. It's the exposure to the top brass. I'm thinking in particular of a visit we made to Wembley back during a period in the 1980s when the FA found endless ways to make the 1966 team feel unappreciated. Banksy, Roger and I were invited to an international with our wives. To get the invitation at all was a turn-up. At half time we'd been instructed to make our way to a hospitality suite. When we got there, we looked around and could see nowhere for us to sit. A couple of tables had no one at them but we were informed that they had been reserved for other people. We were none of us prima donnas demanding special treatment, but if you're a guest you would normally expect to get looked after. It's almost as if no one at the FA could give a shit. They'd bunged us old lags an invite and seemingly that was enough.

The three World Cup winners and two of their wives stood about awkwardly, feeling that something was wrong but not quite knowing what to do about it. Being a little more forceful, my brilliant wife decided to take the initiative. 'We're sitting down here,' she said, pointing at the reserved tables. And we did.

If there had been peanuts, she'd have flicked them at members of the FA.

11

RAY, GEORGE AND BANKSY

For years now, the England squad has been drawn from a small selection of the same old super-rich clubs. It wasn't like that in 1966. Manchester United and Tottenham Hotspur were the glamour names of the decade, and Liverpool and Leeds were rising powers, but back in the day when the First Division was more of a democracy, Alf Ramsey cast his net wide. Nowhere is this more apparent than in the careers of three men at the back: our goalkeeper Gordon Banks, our right back George Cohen and our left back Ray Wilson.

In the 1960s it was not so easy for a player to up sticks and move. The clubs held all the cards, and if they didn't want to sell there wasn't much a player with itchy feet could do about it. As a result, this was an era when the best players were more evenly distributed around the country. Banksy started out in the Third Division at Chesterfield until, proving far too valuable not to cash in, he was sold to Leicester City. They were hardly a fashionable club, but with them he did reach a couple of FA Cup finals, in 1961 and again two years later. As for Ray, although he very much wanted to move to a bigger club, he spent all of his twenties playing for Huddersfield Town, who were in the Second Division when he was first capped. A late transfer to Everton brought him a Cup medal in 1966.

George was Fulham through and through and, despite interest from bigger clubs, was never allowed to leave and so never won anything. More than anyone else in the team, they were men of the people, modest types from humble backgrounds. From their early days each could remember Saturdays where they'd catch the same bus to the game as the fans who were paying to see them play.

I think it's worth asking the question: after we won the World Cup, did my three teammates get the credit they deserved?

Let's start with the full backs. I have a feeling that neither is quite the household name they should be. Bobby Charlton said Ray's tackle was 'as sharp and hard as anything I have ever seen in the game'. George was hailed by no less a figure than George Best as the best right back he ever played against. And yet even at the time, the FA secretary Denis Follows didn't know which full back was which. On the day of the final, he shook Ray by the hand and said, 'Good luck, George.' Ray didn't bother to put him right.

I don't know for sure why they are relatively unsung, but I've got a theory or two. It may be because of that long association both had with less celebrated clubs. Or was it because they were the first of us to retire from football? Perhaps both. Aside from when they played for England, their performances weren't often seen on TV. It would be hard to put together a great highlights reel on YouTube for either of them. But probably it also has something to do with the fact that they played in positions which were then viewed as purely defensive. Full backs didn't make headlines in 1966. They certainly didn't score a lot of goals. Both managed six in their entire careers.

Whatever posterity chooses to remember, Ray and George – like Banksy – were very great players, and we would have been nothing without them. Their job was to make England impregnable. Alf recognised this from the start. Ray, who had played in all four games in the 1962 World Cup in Chile, was Alf's first choice from the off much as Bobby Moore was. Banksy made his debut in 1963 in Alf's second game in charge. George got in a year later after Jimmy Armfield was injured. They were vital building blocks in Alf's rearguard. Jack Charlton didn't complete the back five until 1965.

This is a period when football was changing its spots and Ray, George and Banksy were part of the evolution. Born either side of 1940, all of us learned to play the game at a time when there were such things as wing halves and inside forwards. By the time we finished, those positions on the field of play were relics of a bygone era. The life of a full back changed as much as anyone's, thanks in large part to Alf's decision to do without old-school wingers. In that game-changing win in Madrid in December 1965, the Wingless Wonders were born, sowing confusion in the Spanish defence. 'Their full backs didn't know who to mark,' remembered Ray. 'They were standing there, ball-watching, and we ripped them to bits.'

The primary job of Ray and George was always to defend, and because neither Jack nor especially Mooro were quick out of the blocks, their speed over the turf was essential. But both developed a nose for turning defence into attack. The goal I scored against Argentina came from a Martin Peters cross, but Martin was fed by a positive upfield ball from Ray. Likewise, the goal I set up for Bobby against Portugal: the chip forward for me to chase came from George.

George was immensely powerful – he had a passion for boxing and you could see he might have been handy in the ring. Alf found out for himself exactly how strong he was when playing in a training game in Madrid before that pivotal friendly against Spain. George must have been unsighted when he made a crunching tackle that upended Alf. 'George,' Alf seethed, 'if I had another fucking full back you wouldn't be playing tomorrow.' As I was still a month away from being picked, I only heard about it later. But I find it hard to believe that George didn't apologise and quietly laugh it off as he laughed off everything. He even made light of a furious Alf preventing him from swapping shirts against Argentina. He was the most open, uncomplicated man, and the nicest person you could wish to meet. Everybody I know who crossed paths with him would say the same thing: 'I met George Cohen, he's the loveliest fella I ever met.' Also, Alf would never in a month of Sundays have dropped the best right back in England.

George had less of a reputation for ball-playing subtlety. Not the most reliable crosser of a ball, he felt a bit wounded by a quip from his Fulham teammate Bobby Robson. Bobby once suggested that in his career George had hit more photo-graphers than Frank Sinatra. I'd like to leap to his defence. In my first time in the squad, weeks after that game in Madrid, England played Poland at Goodison Park and George shim-mied past two defenders to set up the equaliser with a clever chip from the outside of his boot. At the end of it was Mooro, whose towering header was his first of only two international goals. And anyone who rewatches the final can see that George had a very good game. He looked after Lothar Emmerich at the back and, further up the field, helped Bally tear Karl-Heinz Schnellinger to pieces.

Over on the other flank, there was Ray. To the world-class players we had in the spine of the team – Banks, Moore, R. Charlton, Greaves – I would always add the name of Ray Wilson. He was a brilliant defender, very good in the air, fit, quick and tough. Whereas George was stocky and strong, Ray was as lean and swift as a whippet. His entry into football was very different too. George had the support of his family. Although his parents could have used the regular income when their son left school, they urged him not to learn a trade but to seize his chance when Fulham offered him an apprenticeship at 15. Ray was the son of a miner. His mother – who named him Ramon after the Hollywood pin-up Ramon Novarro – died when he was 15. When he was eventually scouted by Bill Shankly, then the manager of Huddersfield, Ray was working nights in a railway carriage repair yard. He was signed as an amateur at 18.

Ray would go on to change the way full backs were perceived. He started out playing on the left wing but Shankly had the bright idea of switching him. The pace Ray needed to get past the right back was now used to stop the right wing getting past him. 'It was a fluke, me moving to left back,' he said late in life. 'Previous to that, the full backs were all as slow as could be. They were all 6ft 2in, 6ft 3in, and it took them 10 minutes to turn around. Bloody wingers were flying past them. I started playing there and they thought, "Ooh, that's a good idea." Well it is, isn't it?' He would go on to have a strange time of it commuting between the Second Division and international football. 'As soon as I got to that level I felt comfortable,' he once said. 'The only problem was that some weeks I'd be playing against Brazil at Wembley and three days later turning out at Scunthorpe or Lincoln.'

He won his first cap in 1960, putting him in the same vintage as other players in the 1966 squad – Ron Springett, Jimmy Armfield, Ron Flowers, John Connelly. In fact, he only just made it through boot camp at Lilleshall. He'd done his back in badly enough that he couldn't lift his arm to shave. As his roommate, Bobby Charlton had to do it for him.

That illustrates just how comfortable the two were with each other. Neither was given to making a lot of noise or drawing attention to himself. In Ray's case, that could change slightly whenever he had a drink in him. Then his quirky side would come out. The day after the opening game against Uruguay, when we visited Pinewood Studios, Alf gave us permission to sip a single lager but Ray somehow managed to get his hands on a lot more. It quickened his tongue. Banksy remembers him talking to Yul Brynner, who told him he was going to be starring in *The King and I* in Newcastle. 'What're they calling it up there, then?' asked Ray. '*The King and Why Aye?*'

He didn't say much but when he did his words had a tang to them. It was Ray who, before the quarter-final, referred to the Argentine captain as the Rat. He'd played against Argentina twice already so maybe knew what was coming down the pipe. He was the coolest person on the pitch when Rattín was arguing about his dismissal. In those long minutes, Ray simply sat on the ball and waited.

The mystery of Ray's disastrous mistake in the final will always be just that. It remains inexplicable. For some reason, he gifted West Germany a goal. In the ninth minute, Sigi Held lumped a hopeful ball on a diagonal towards the right-hand side of the box. It was a nothing cross, with no whip or power – Ray later called it 'a Third Division ball' – and there was no one near him as it drifted down. It's possible he had too much time to think. Bobby was in front of him and it must have been him he was aiming for, but the ball somehow flopped off his head straight into the path of Helmut Haller, who probably couldn't believe his luck. He didn't control it particularly well, but before Bobby or Mooro or Ray could close him down he managed to get off a mishit waft of a shot. Jack didn't react in time to intercept it and Banksy couldn't reach it so the ball bobbled almost slowly into the far corner. One–nil, thanks to a succession of accidents and system failures. Ever afterwards Ray was mystified. 'That was an awful mistake,' he said in the documentary *How England Won the World Cup '66* we all contributed to 40 years later. 'I mistimed it pretty badly. It was pretty disappointing. But if you're a defender and you can't live with making mistakes then you wouldn't turn out in the second half.' After, Alf said to him, 'That's the first mistake you've made for me in four years.' Banksy wasn't happy either. He absolutely loathed letting in goals.

The story of Gordon Banks is a slightly separate case. At the 1970 World Cup, when faced with Pelé in the group match against Brazil, he would seal his reputation with probably the greatest save in the history of the game. But in the 1960s goalkeepers were not thought of as stars in the same way as the great attacking players. Clubs didn't spend big money on them. And there was certainly no such thing as goalkeeping coaches. So as a young man making his way in the game, Banksy decided to devise his own training programme and, basically, to coach himself.

In doing so, he more or less invented the modern concept of goalkeeping. I remember him telling me about all this when we got to know each other better. He was already blessed with a great deal of natural upper-body strength and lower-limb power, built up in early years working as a coal-bagger, hod-carrier and bricklayer. Everything else was the product of deep thought and hard work. At Leicester, he used to do all the same exercises as the outfield players. He questioned this, and when nothing was done about it he shrugged and created his own drills instead. This took vision and a hell of a lot of determination. He was so dedicated that for a long time at Leicester he would do extra training on Sundays, and got volunteers to help him. Over the years he came up with a regime that worked on all aspects of goalkeeping: handling, positioning, footwork, clearances, every conceivable type of shot-stopping from high to low, long range and close range. He made a great study of the science of angles, minimising the options of attackers preparing to shoot, and arranging defenders in front of him to enlarge his field of vision. He made himself the boss of the box. According to Banksy, he even developed no fewer than seven different types of punch. That must be more than Muhammad Ali had.

I had already played against Banksy at club level. It was only when I came into the England squad that I saw how dedicated he was to his craft on the training pitch. Even when the game meant nothing, he was incredibly hard to beat. He was so committed that there was always the possibility of injury. Bobby

Charlton once asked him about this. 'Without doing what I did today,' he replied, 'with all the risks, I simply couldn't do my job.' (He was also quite a useful outfield player in five-a-sides, which wasn't the case with most keepers back then.)

England let in three goals at the 1966 World Cup and Banksy was pissed off about all of them. The first was Eusébio's penalty in the dying minutes of the semi-final. Banksy knew exactly which way to dive until Bally got into his head, signalling that he was certain Eusébio was going to go the other way. I seem to remember he gave Bally a piece of his mind.

Off the pitch, Banksy was very gentle and softly spoken with a lovely smile. He always had a joke for you. I remember once when we were playing away and had dinner booked in the hotel after the game. To get to the small dining room set aside for the squad we had to walk through a large dining room where a pianist was singing into a microphone. He was really quite loud. I was just behind Banksy as we walked in single file past this pianist when he stopped.

'Do you do requests?' he said.

'Yeah,' the pianist replied.

'Can you play "Far Away"?'

It may be because Banksy was such a physically imposing man that I never realised when I played with or against him how catlike he was in his approach. Only later on, watching clips of him, did I come to appreciate his sleek and darting style of movement. Without any shadow of a doubt he is the greatest goalkeeper I've ever seen. He was the best then, and to my mind no one has come along to surpass him. That's not to say he was the most spectacular. You would never see him waving his hands like an air traffic controller. The acrobatic displays that some foreign keepers went in for weren't his style at all. He wasn't one to show off and didn't see it as his job to be an entertainer. In his memoir he told a funny story about the England game for which I was called up to the squad for the first time, in January 1966, when Roger Hunt drew a spectacular flying save from the Polish keeper, who gave away a corner. The whole of Goodison Park erupted in generous applause. Then a Polish striker shot from the same sort of distance, and Banksy, who had got himself into the correct position, simply reached up and caught it just below the bar. That was him all over: no fuss, no theatrics, just skill and technique. No one clapped. They nicknamed him Banks of England for a reason: he could be trusted.

If it was great to know that such a titan was behind me at international level, it was a different story when he was in front of me at club level. Banksy was responsible for the worst moment in my entire career. West Ham were playing Stoke in the semi-final of the 1971–2 League Cup over two legs. Up there, I scored a penalty and we won. We then came back to Upton Park. We were losing 1–0 when late in the game Harry Redknapp was brought down in the box. I lined up to take the penalty, reasonably confident as I had beaten Banksy from the spot the previous week. If I scored we were in the final. I gave it an almighty thump and it was flying to Banksy's right under the bar. But he stuck out an arm, it hit his wrist and sailed over. The accuracy he needed to intercept a ball travelling so fast, and the strength in his wrist to block the power of the shot – well, it suits me to call it a fluke. We had two more replays, because back then nothing was decided on shootouts, which took almost a month and then they knocked us out. And then they won the competition – Stoke's only major trophy. I often teased him about the save. 'Forget all this crap about this great save you made against Brazil,' I'd tell him, 'the most important one was against me because it got you through to the final. The save against Pelé made absolutely no difference to the result of the game. We still got beat. If you're on the losing side it don't count!'

Banksy would talk about the save too. He noticed that I used to take penalties with a longish run-up and generally shoot inside the post to the keeper's right. 'You run up exactly the same way so I knew it was going to go that way.' In other words, I had a tell, and he told me what it was. It was too late to do anything about it, as we'd both retired by then.

At the end of that season, we both played our last games for England. That summer of 1972, West Ham decided to sell me and Banksy was instrumental in persuading me to join him at Stoke. We might have had a couple more enjoyable seasons playing together every week but that October he had the car accident that blinded him in one eye and ended his career at the top level.

Afterwards, Ray slipped away from the game without a backward glance, training to become an undertaker in his father-in-law's business. This surely says something about the stoicism of the man. George also needed immense reserves of inner strength when for many years he fought off cancer. As for Banksy, his body eventually gained the upper hand. He summed up the journey that he and it had been on together in a wonderful gag he used to deliver as an after-dinner speaker. 'I've broken most bones in my fingers and thumbs and wrists.

A knuckle disappeared in 1968. I had a metal pin in my knee, a plate in my elbow. I've had two hip replacements. I'm blind in one eye. Yet I still get some fucking idiot coming up to me and asking if I still play.'

12
GOLF DAYS

T his is a football story, yes. But it also involves another sport: golf. If it was football that brought us together, it was golf that kept us together.

Those 11 players were selected by Alf because he thought we were the best men for the job. Ever since, we have been yoked together in the public mind. But how well did we really know one another? It's natural for any football fan to assume that we all grew instantly close, although this is to romanticise how a football team works. We did have a great mutual respect. But we might go for quite long periods without being in touch.

This is part of the dynamic of an international football squad. If you're selected to play for your country, you meet up, you train, you play, you go back to your club. Players come, players go. You know them from playing against them at club level, but you don't know them anything like as intimately as you do the teammates you spend your working week with. Because there was far less movement between clubs in the transfer market in the 1960s, you could spend many years in the company of the same people. West Ham's three World Cup winners played together every week for the best part of a decade until Martin Peters left for Spurs in 1970.

With England it was different. From the day I was first called into an England squad in January 1966, I spent time with a revolving cast of footballers and some I barely exchanged a word with. That's not to say that there was any disharmony. It's just that you're there to do a job: to represent your country, if selected.

I got on well enough with pretty much everyone in the 1966 squad. I will quietly admit there was one player among us who was not generally liked, although the name of this individual could be extracted from me only under torture, and probably not even then. What position did he play? Not telling. Was he from the north or the south or somewhere in between? Pass. Is he still with us? I couldn't possibly say. But this is perfectly normal. In any walk of life you have to work with people that you don't see eye to eye with – I certainly did when I went into business. So long as the job gets done, it doesn't matter. Football is full of stories of players who didn't get on and yet made magic on the pitch. At Liverpool, in Bill Shankly's team of the early 1970s, Tommy Smith and Emlyn Hughes famously hated each other. In Kenny Dalglish's squad in the 1980s there were several enmities on the go. What about Manchester United? Bobby Charlton, Denis Law and George Best seemed telepathic when they played but otherwise were chalk, cheese and Chablis. And let's not get started on Teddy Sheringham and Andy Cole, who combined superbly on the pitch but never exchanged a single word off it.

I'm relieved to say I experienced none of that. I don't tend to fall out with people. At the same time, although I have so much admiration for the 1966 team, then and now, there was no particular individual who I grew especially close to. I loved them all. But when we were players, I didn't necessarily know them that deeply as people. I knew them as footballers.

Even after we were brought together for one reunion or another, we didn't always have the opportunity to spend much time in one another's company. One of the glitziest gatherings was a testimonial dinner at the Café Royal in London. It took place in 1974, on the anniversary of our 1966 triumph. That month Franz Beckenbauer and West Germany won the World Cup in a tournament England had not qualified for, earning Alf Ramsey the sack and a not very golden handshake from the FA. The dinner was held to raise £10,000 to add to his pay-off. Most of the 1966 squad were there – I can't remember for sure, but I suspect Jimmy Greaves was one of the three absentees – as well as many other players selected by Alf during his time with England. We all put on dickey bows and the World Cup winners posed for press photos with Alf at the front clutching a replica of the Jules Rimet trophy. Les Cocker and Harold Shepherdson were there too. Looking back at them 50 years on, it seems to have been a very jolly gathering, although there was a slight stench of bitterness in the air at Alf's perceived mistreatment by the FA.

We were wheeled out on several such occasions, all of us or some of us, often when there was another World Cup and the broadcasters and newspapers wanted to hear how once upon a time it was won by England. Once we went to Germany for a reunion with our opponents. Even the ref was there!

Some of the earliest reunions were on the pitch. In the era before massive salaries, clubs would arrange a testimonial game for a senior pro to earn him a few extra quid. It was a way for fans to express their gratitude for that player's loyalty over the years. After nearly a decade in the first team, West Ham organised one for me in 1971. 'Some achieve greatness; others have it thrust upon them,' a local journalist wrote in the match programme. Shakespeare, I believe! I was incredibly flattered by the turnout. We played against an all-star European XI. Jimmy had just hung up his boots but generously came out of retirement to play. There was only him and Mooro from the England squad, but it was instead a reunion with opponents from the 1966 World Cup. The scratch all-stars included Eusébio and Simões, who were semi-finalists for Portugal, and Willi Schulz and Uwe Seeler from West Germany's finalists. I've got the match report in my scrapbook collection.

There was a more familiar look to reunions later in the decade, when a lot of the 1966 team had retired and were more available for such get-togethers. Alan Mullery became a popular member of the England set-up when, in 1970, he took Nobby Stiles's place at the base of the midfield. He scored the first goal in the quarter-final against West Germany – the game that got away. Eventually he moved from Spurs back to Fulham and encouraged Mooro to join him there. They had a lovely sentimental outing to Wembley in 1975 when Fulham, then in the Second Division, played West Ham. We all came along for Alan in March 1976 when a very good Scotland XI took on a Rest of Great Britain XI. My memory is hazy of the actual day. It says in the programme that Mooro, Jimmy, Alan Ball and Norman Hunter from the 1966 squad played for the Rest of GB team (which strangely contained two Italians). But there's a lovely picture in the dressing room at Craven Cottage of the whole 1966 team bar Ray Wilson and Jack Charlton. We're all in football kit apart from George Cohen, who would have been unable to play for health reasons. Alf is there too in a three-piece suit, looking happy. The mystery of who among us actually played is probably lost in the mists. The point is, we're all smiling and it looks like another enjoyable gathering. And it would have been. We were always delighted to see one another.

We definitely did all play at Martin Peters's testimonial a couple of years later. He ended up at Norwich City for five years from 1975 and became so popular that the fans voted him one of the best players in the club's history. The names listed on the team sheet that day were as follows: Springett, Stiles, Hollins, Greaves, J. Charlton, Moore, Ball, Hunt, R. Charlton, Hurst, Peters. No wonder the game attracted a crowd of 18,000. Our bones were a little creakier, our speed of movement maybe not what it was, but all the same, a dozen years on from the World Cup final that's quite a turnout. That we all wanted to support him shows how much we thought of Martin, but it's also typical of the camaraderie that would continue throughout our lives. Only John Hollins, just 20 when he won a lone cap in 1967, wasn't from the 1966 squad. With Ray and George unavailable, I've absolutely no recollection of who played at full back. Jimmy, only months after taking the momentous decision to swear off alcohol, played his heart out and refused to accept any expenses.

The biggest and most important reunion on the pitch took place on 29 July 1985. It was brought about after a fire broke out in a condemned old stand at Valley Parade, the home of

Bradford City, during the last game of the season. Claiming the lives of 56 football fans, with hundreds more casualties, it was the first of the three big tragedies in the 1980s, succeeded by Heysel and Hillsborough, that changed the way football is watched in England. A disaster appeal fund was instantly set up and, to contribute to it, the entire England team from 1966 turned out at Elland Road, 19 years on from our big day. Our opponents, who generously flew in that morning, were a West German team containing seven of our old opponents: Tilkowski, Beckenbauer, Schulz, Held, Seeler, Overath and Emmerich. The right back Schnellinger was one of the absentees – maybe he couldn't face the thought of having to mark Bally again.

By this time, we really were starting to show our age. Our movement was slower and we were carrying a bit of timber around the midriff, apart from Mooro of course. Nobby played with his teeth in. Ray, after seven knee ops, trotted out for a five-minute cameo. George lasted slightly longer. Even Roger went off at half time. The Germans looked quite tasty and little Seeler seemed to have lost none of his canny appetite for goal. We were behind at half time but managed to run out 6–4 winners. The match highlights on YouTube testify that some of the old skills were intact. Bobby was letting off his missiles from distance, Bally scored with a crafty chip, Martin cut holes through defences, Banksy with his one good eye threw himself about, Jack's long legs were still slide-tackling. Oh, and I got a hattrick. A cutting from my scrapbook sounds a note of nostalgic romance: 'Because of their manners as well as their skills,' wrote Brian James in the *Daily Mail*, 'because of the way they achieved great triumph and then lived their remaining sporting lives without disgrace, it is very easy for us to believe them to be the last of the heroes.' I couldn't possibly comment …

For the most part, we would meet up and then disappear back into our regular lives. The pattern for years was that we only ever got together when someone invited us to remember the big day. In the 1990s, an agent/manager called David Davies got some of us together to do a nationwide speaking tour. He'd perm four or five from George, Banksy, Bally, Roger, Jack, Martin and me, and book us into a venue. We'd answer questions from our host, sitting with us onstage, and then do a Q&A session with the audience. Memories of 1966 had faded and these shows didn't always attract a massive crowd. Once, in Newcastle, only 13 people turned up so the performers and the audience reconvened to the bar and did the show there instead.

Over the many years they continued to happen, the thing that all these gatherings had in common was that they were organised by other people. We got together because someone else was paying us to, or because we were helping to raise money for a good cause. We were always happy to turn up but they required us to be on our best behaviour. And there was always an audience. I could joke and lark about with my teammates all day long. Humour and fun were an essential part of who we were behind closed doors. But on these occasions we were in a more ambassadorial role and mucking about would be looked upon as inappropriate. So we had to keep a straight face.

Take the cruises we were regularly invited on from the mid-1990s. The basic payment was the cruise, which is not a form of remuneration in kind I generally agree with. You're on parade, mingling with passengers morning, noon and night.

We were also required to do two or three Q&As with an audience. Imagine a cruise company offering the current England team a trip in lieu of payment! They happened every so often and we accepted because it gave us an opportunity to see each other. One of them managed to get nine of us all together. There's a wonderful picture of us in our red England shirts on deck with the captain. Some of us were more comfortable with the glad-handing than others. Ray was so conscientious at moving among the passengers that we awarded him the honorary title of chief mingler. He was a lovely character who got on with people. Because the ship's passengers skewed towards retirees, maybe one of us even teased him about drumming up custom for his undertaker's business in Huddersfield.

It was Jack who suggested we move the goalposts. In 1996, we had been yanked back into the public eye thanks to the euphoria of England's near miss when hosting the Euros. Eyes were upon us again. Nobby's dancing even made it into the lyrics of 'Three Lions', with the whole of Wembley singing about football coming home after three decades of hurt every time England advanced. We had all been so close in 1966, and most of us carried that through to the four years to 1970. We got on, but there was no structure enabling us to continue enjoying one another's company. Jack's idea was that we should get together under our own steam, without anyone else watching, and we should bring along our wives. Most importantly, we would be gathering in private.

So, in 1998 Martin and I organised the first 1966 reunion. The plan we came up with was to invite all the members of the squad, and their wives, to attend a golf day with two evenings

– one before the golf, one after – when we'd all get together for drinks and dinner. Most of us enjoyed a round. The old pros would go out with their clubs and play 18 holes, while the wives did their own thing.

It was very important to include the whole squad. We never wanted there to be a divide between them and the 11 of us who played in the final. So those people who happened to play only one game, or didn't get on the pitch at all, were invited too. This was before we were all on email, so it took a bit of legwork, but the response was very good right away, and a very large number came.

The first golf day was at the Foxhills club near Weybridge in Surrey, which I knew because we lived nearby and I played there now and again. From the winning team, only Banksy couldn't make it for some reason. Ray came even though he wasn't a golfer, but he walked around the course instead.

We had a fantastic time and agreed that we should try and do it every year. So it was in the golf days that the members of the England squad got to know one another all over again on our own terms. Every year, every time we got back together, it felt as if we hadn't been apart. That was the beauty of the relationship when we were playing together. There was an immediate sense of warmth and togetherness. And when we met up in the evenings the conversation didn't linger on the significance of what we achieved. We may have been known to the public as great players, great teammates and great characters, but we got together as just ordinary guys who chatted about everyday things.

Our wives, who had been segregated into a separate room at the Royal Garden Hotel on the night of the final, mostly

came too. To us – if not to Alf! – they were a fundamental part
of what happened in 1966, and it was important that it wasn't
just a boys' club. Judith was already thick as thieves with Kathy
Peters. But now we spent time with Pat Charlton and Norma
Charlton, Ursula Banks, Pat Wilson, Daphne Cohen, Kay
Stiles, Lesley Ball, Barbara Springett, Roger Hunt's second
wife Rowan, Norman Hunter's wife Sue, Peter Bonetti's second
wife Kay, while Ian Callaghan brought quite a few different
companions along. After John Connelly died in 2012, we made
sure to ask his widow Sandra to the next golf day and she was
delighted. I've a strong memory from that year of us sitting up
into the very small hours with her, Roger and Rowan, Cally
and his partner.

That first year, Judith organised a trip for the wives to
the gardens at RHS Wisley. Later, as we moved up and down
the country, there would be outings to a fabric museum, to
the Wedgwood Museum, to Bettys Café Tea Rooms. I won't
name either of the parties involved, but one year a wife who
was hosting proposed taking the ladies to see a statue of her
husband. Another wife was a bit sniffy about this option, and
noses were put out of joint. But according to Judith, who grew
to know and like all the wives, 'They were all very ordinary nice
women who were easy to get on with from the start. No one
wanted to stand out. No one was vying to be top dog.'

After the first two golf days, Martin and I passed the baton
on to others in the group to organise reunions in other parts of
the country. So we met at every point of the compass: Lytham
St Annes on the Lancashire coast, Dale Hill in East Sussex,
Acton Trussell in Staffordshire. The atmosphere was always

relaxed and there were plenty of laughs, but the get-togethers were meaningful too. I won't make any great claims for the standard of the golf. We'd play two-balls or three-balls, depending on how many of us were there. They were friendly games. Not many of us would have been much cop on the pro-am circuit. Roger was much the most able golfer – he played off something like seven. Banksy was also great. Those two used to play each other a lot when they sat together on the pools panel. Martin wasn't bad. I don't think Jack was that great. Nor were George or Nobby. I was so-so, golf never being something I was fanatical about. I didn't practise my pitching and putting the way I worked at my near-post heading, and never acquired a genuine handicap.

My favourite golf story involving my old teammates was actually not part of these annual reunions. Instead, it took place in Australia, where for several years on the trot Judith and I used to go on holiday as guests of my friend Terry Hopley. He had a house at Sanctuary Cove on the Gold Coast, and kept inviting me to come out. 'No, I'm busy,' I'd say. 'Come out,' he'd say the next year. 'No, I'm busy.' Eventually he said, 'If you don't come out soon we'll both be fucking dead.' That got my attention. So we went. One year we found out that Bally and Roger were going to be out there at the same time, and we decided to meet up for a round of golf.

We made up a four-ball. On the way round we decided to wind Roger up. It was Bally's idea, being the wicked little so-and-so that he was. Thanks to Terry's local knowledge, we knew there was a hole on the course where, when you walk up to the tee, you're not sure which way to drive off as it's not perfectly clear where the fairway is. I was partnering Terry. To make certain it worked we needed to ensure that Roger and Bally won the previous hole so he would tee off first. So Terry whacked his final putt almost off the green. 'That was fucking stupid,' I muttered. 'You could have conned him a bit more subtly.' Roger didn't seem to notice. We moved on to the next hole where the three of us made a great show of practising our swings in unison. Roger naturally assumed that the direction we were preparing to drive in was the one indicated by the way we were flicking our clubs. He sets himself, does a practice swing of his own and sends not a bad drive flying down completely the wrong fairway. Then the rest of us all stood up and, one by one, turned through 90 degrees and drove off in a different direction.

He didn't take it too badly.

After Martin, who I knew so well, I find it hard to pick out anyone from the 1966 team that I was closest to. But if I had to choose one, it would be Roger. He was such a decent man and I couldn't have enjoyed his company more. Judith and I visited him and Rowan where they lived in Lancashire. We had other evenings with Bobby and Norma, or Jack and Pat.

Jack was always fantastic company, though you never knew what he was going to do next. For the 40th anniversary of the World Cup in July 2006, we did a big event at the Bournemouth International Centre. The players all shared the takings from the box office and we also sold memorabilia. Beforehand there was a dinner where Jack went rogue and started inviting the audience up to get autographs. A long queue soon formed and it took so long that half the people who'd bought theatre tickets asked for their money back.

That event was organised by Terry Baker, who would become my agent. He also got us doing these big signing sessions at the NEC in Birmingham. They were like *Star Trek* conventions, except with footballers from stardate 1966. They were very successful. People would happily wait in line for hours to get our autographs on posters, photos and other mementos. Ray once calculated that he made more money from these events than he did in the entirety of his playing career.

They'd last all weekend, so on the Saturday night we'd go out to dinner. Not always together, mind. Some of us had a stronger hankering for Little Chef than others. But in 2006 there was a fancy restaurant opening so Jack and Nobby were persuaded to join George, Terry and me. We even talked them into sampling the wine instead of necking beer as usual. The problem was that they knocked it back as if it was beer. Later that night, Jack spent two hours trying to find his room. Nobby couldn't as he was incapable of independent navigation or even movement, so we carried him back to his room and put him in bed. He was out cold. There was a bit of worry that he'd swallow his false teeth. Rather than undress him we decided just to remove his jacket and trousers. One of our party got the jacket off and was about to undo his trousers when Nobby opened his eyes and, in that Mancunian accent of his, went, 'Fook off.'

The only downside to spending time with Jack was it was quite a job to get him to put his hand in his pocket. In fact, I don't think I ever managed it. 'I'm a wealthy lad, me,' he'd say. Bless him, though, he more than paid me back one year. When I was working in the insurance business we sometimes laid on

CHAPTER 12

treats for clients to help keep the relationship in good health. In
1995, a couple of them expressed a wish to go fishing. I've never
known one end of a rod from another, but I knew a man who
did. So I got hold of Jack and invited him to join three clients
of mine on a fishing trip to Ireland. Even though there was
nothing in it for him but a free trip, he was delighted to accept
and obviously he was in his element. My clients, who found him
wonderfully down to earth, couldn't believe their luck that I'd
managed to land such a big fish.

I wasn't there every time my teammates met up. I must
have been otherwise engaged when seven of our team were
invited to 11 Downing Street by the then Chancellor of the
Exchequer Gordon Brown for a reception attended by many of
our German opponents, including Franz Beckenbauer and my
old chum Hans Tilkowski. Then in 2011 Hans and I were both
guests at my most unusual World Cup final reunion, which took
place in Baku, the capital of Azerbaijan. I was invited to join
the celebrations to mark 100 years of football in the country.
It was an amusing idea to pair Hans and me at the ceremony
because, let's face it, the most famous Azerbaijani in football is
not a player but a linesman. Tofiq Bahramov, who made what is
surely the most lengthily debated line call in the game's history, is
a fairly significant person in my life. If I'd only scored two goals
instead of three I bet I'd have enjoyed less than two-thirds the
amount of attention. I owe the Russian-speaking Bahramov for
confidently informing Gottfried Dienst, the German-speaking
Swiss ref, that my shot had clearly crossed the line. Arguably,
all England owes him too. I gladly accepted and was delighted
to learn that Bahramov is a national hero who, after Azerbaijan

gained its independence in 1991, had the national stadium named after him.

Hans and I were shown an absolutely gigantic statue of Bahramov, and posed for a photo in front of it with the great man's son. I don't speak a word of German, and Hans's English wasn't up to much either, so communication was nearly as basic as it was between the officials on the pitch in 1966. I could have asked Sepp Blatter, who was also there, though I wouldn't have trusted him to act as anyone's interpreter. On the couple of occasions I met Hans at functions in Germany, we had a more reliable translator in the shape of Hans's daughter Susanne. We became friendly enough that one year, when we couldn't find the right spare parts for our German-made toilet, Judith rang Susanne. The daughter of the 1966 West Germany goalkeeper ordered them for us and got them sent to Cheltenham. So the Tilkowskis have clearly forgiven the Hursts. Strangely enough, the one topic Hans and I never touched on was the FAQ of whether the ball had crossed the line.

Meanwhile, the golf days continued very happily for nearly two decades. Jimmy never came, though, because, as a recovering alcoholic, he found it uncomfortable to attend social occasions oiled by drinking.

In 2013, 15 years on from the first one, we had a press photocall, this time at Brocton Hall in Staffordshire. Twelve of us were there, including both Charltons. Staffordshire proved a handy choice as it was relatively easy for everyone to get to from north and south. In 2016, on the 50th anniversary of 1966, we were back there for what we didn't necessarily know was to be our last reunion. But we had a hunch. The numbers were dwindling. Although he lived in South Africa, George Eastham made the trip several times and that year gave a very moving speech in which he thanked the winning team for including all those squad members who had been somewhat forgotten by history.

Then when we came to think about doing another, we realised that we had met for the final time.

Not that long ago, I had a hip operation and decided that was enough golf for me. I haven't missed it. I had my best day on a football pitch with the boys of '66, and my best days on the golf course with them too.

13

NOBBY
AND BALLY

It's a fact of football history that I scored the most contro-versial goal in almost a century of World Cups. That's 22 competitions and, if the maths is right, 964 matches. The sight of an orange leather ball thudding down off the underside of the bar at Wembley Stadium must be singed onto the eyeballs of millions of England fans, and a lot of German ones too.

But how much is remembered about the move that led up to it?

If you rewind from my shot on the turn, you've got a cross to the near post from Alan Ball out on the right. It's perfectly weighted, bouncing once just in front of me. Bally doesn't look up or to his left. His eyes are on the ball as he prepares to swing his right foot. He knows, because I've told him and told him, that I like crosses fired in towards the near post. So without checking to see that I'm there, that's where he hits it with one touch.

First, though, he has to get to the ball. We're well into extra time and no one has covered more of the Wembley pitch than Bally. He's been up and down, he's been left and right. He's been everywhere, all afternoon. By rights he should be half dead with exhaustion, but rewind a couple more seconds and those little legs of his are still on the go as he gallops towards the right-hand corner flag where the ball is slowing up, as if waiting for him to reach it. His energy is astonishing.

Now spool back a bit more. The pass he's chasing has been dinked over the head of Schnellinger. The German left back is world class but, thanks to Bally, he has had a horrible afternoon, and now for the umpteenth time he's having to chase this pesky ginger kid who won't stop running. It's such a lovely pass, flighted from the centre circle just inside our half and angled into empty space. It comes from the boot of … well, anyone would think it must be one of the Bobbys. It's in their style, calm and certain, probing and accurate.

But no, it's from our little enforcer Nobby Stiles. Nobby is extremely short-sighted and missing all his front teeth and barely looks like any sort of footballer. Even his kit doesn't seem to quite fit him. Also he's come through a torrid ordeal in this World Cup. He's been ripped apart by the press, accused of playing dangerously to the extent that the FA even asked Alf not to pick him. Alf called their bluff: if he goes, he replied, I go too. And here Nobby is in extra time of the final, stroking the ball around like an artist. Like a Bobby.

One pass. One cross. One shot. And thanks to a linesman from the Soviet Union, one goal that has been disputed ever since.

Nobby was our best player in the semi-final. Bally was our best player in the final. When I joined the England squad earlier that year, aside from Bobby Moore and Martin Peters they were the only players I knew – Nobby from Under 17 level, both of them from the Under 23s. Together, they formed the heart and soul of our team. None was more loyal to the cause, or more grateful to be there. Both won their first full caps just over a year out from the World Cup. Both no taller than five foot six, both weighing only ten stone, they became two peas in a pod, an inseparable pair of Bash Street Kids.

No wonder Alf had the idea to billet them in the same room at Hendon Hall Hotel. They were at the heart of the endless card games we played morning, noon and night to while away the hours. There's a snap from 1966 of Nobby and Bally sitting opposite Roger Hunt and me in our shirts and ties as we played cards on the team bus. The game we played was called Seven. To win, you had to collect four of one card and three of another. (Four and three. I'm not saying this was an omen but those two numbers turned out well for England and Hurst in the final.) Nobby and Bally took competition to the next level. Whenever they played, whichever one of them lost had to be servant to the other for the rest of the day.

On the pitch, Alf wanted both of them to be servants to Bobby Charlton. He said as much one day at Roehampton. 'Has either of you got a dog?' he asked, drawing them aside. Bally said he had. 'You know when you throw a ball it chases after it? That's what I want you both to do for Bobby. Win the ball and give it to him.'

Bally put it even more colourfully as an after-dinner speaker. 'Me and Nobby knew what our job was. So off we'd go, snorting, scratching, tackling, fighting, Nobby occasionally biting, but we'd get it back, and we'd give it him again.' Whenever all three of them played in midfield, the stats show that England became impossible to beat. Nobby and Bally were capped together 18 times for England, and it wasn't until two years later, and that grudge match against Scotland in 1967, that the midfield trio tasted defeat for the only time. I think they were so passionate about playing for England because, for different reasons, neither of them expected to. Each had a bumpy path to the top.

Nobby's problem was optical. He had astigmatism and whenever he wasn't on a football pitch he wore glasses with heavy frames and pebble-thick lenses. It was so unusual to see footballers arriving at or leaving the ground in glasses that they became an essential part of who he was. Even when playing other sports. From one of the press days at Roehampton there are snaps of the squad larking about at a game of cricket. Two show Nobby. He's either a left-handed batter, or a right-handed wrist spinner, but he's never without his specs on.

In the circumstances it seems a miracle that he ever made it. In fact, he was good enough as a boy to be selected for England Schoolboys, and like Martin Peters had a very early experience of playing at Wembley. Yet for a long time he admitted his eye problem to no one. He must have feared that owning up to poor eyesight might spell the end of his career. So when he played he could literally lose sight of the player he was marking. Once, he even mislaid his dentures on a muddy pitch, and from then on decided to take them out before the game. It was his teammate at Manchester United, the goalkeeper Harry Gregg, who diagnosed the problem when he spotted that Nobby was laying down the wrong cards in a card game. The club sent Nobby to a specialist and he emerged into a bright sharp world seen through new contact lenses. These made all the difference. Suddenly he could identify the faces of everyone on the pitch, and had more than a vague idea of the flight of the ball through the air.

The following season he became a permanent fixture in Man U's first team and was selected to play for England at Under 23 level. The first game – the one he had to miss a vital league fixture to play in – was against a Scotland side in Aberdeen. Nobby managed to leave the fluid for his contacts behind so he was back to playing in a fog. At half time, Alf gave him the specific instruction to take out the Chelsea winger Charlie Cooke, who was causing problems. The often told story is that Nobby timed his tackle to perfection, went in hard and got his man. Only it was a case of mistaken identity. He'd upended the wrong Scot. The one he got was the ginger powder keg Billy Bremner. 'What the fuck do you think you're doing?!' shouted Norman Hunter, who happened to be Bremner's clubmate at Leeds.

Alf was impressed enough to give him his first full cap two months later, in April 1965. He was still only 22. This was also against Scotland, but at home. Before picking him, Alf was keen to know if Nobby had it in him to set aside club solidarity and clatter into Man United's star striker Denis Law if the need arose. Alf consulted Wilf McGuinness, his Under 23s assistant who also coached at Man U. Could Nobby nobble Law? 'No fucking danger,' came the reply. Denis made it easier for Nobby, who in the spirit of friendliness tried to shake hands with his teammate before the game. 'Fuck off, you wee English bastard,' said Denis. And knowing Denis, I imagine he wouldn't have been even half-joking. It was all the motivation Nobby needed. In that game, England were reduced by injuries to nine men. There being no subs, Bobby Charlton fetched up as emergency right back, but they held on for a 2–2 draw thanks in part to Nobby's heroics.

Incidentally, this was Jack Charlton's first cap too. No game could have been better suited to blooding him or Nobby. England now had two players at the heart of the team who maybe weren't the prettiest, but loved a scrap. They were so good at getting stuck in they often could be heard to give each other an earful. A scowling Jack would address Nobby as 'you little bastard' and a gobby Nobby would come right back at Jack with 'you big twat'. One day on the training pitch at Lilleshall, they nearly came to blows until Alf parted them in that head-masterly way of his. (Bally brilliantly took the piss out of Jack too. Jack in turn affectionately called him 'you little shit'.)

Not that Nobby's place at the base of the midfield was set in stone. When I won my first cap in early 1966 at home to West Germany, it was in basically the line-up that would win the World Cup, especially after Ray Wilson came on at half time. The only missing piece of the jigsaw was Martin Peters. Norman Hunter, winning his second cap, played in central defence as he did with Jack for Leeds, and Bobby Moore was moved into the anchoring role. So Nobby was relieved of his defensive duties and shuffled into an attacking role. He even stabbed in the winner from less than a yard out. Part of me wishes it had been me rather than him who got that goal because it would have settled my nerves a lot. It turned out to be the only time Nobby would score for England.

Nobby was a far more technical and creative player than people ever gave him credit for. 'A football game was for Nobby always an open book,' reckoned George Cohen. 'He could read every nuance of it, and nobody needed to point this out to Ramsey.' But it was his toughness that Alf valued above other qualities. Where that toughness came from is anyone's guess. Some aggressive players could have quite a fearsome aura off the pitch too. From the same era, you might not fancy bumping into hard-as-nails Dave Mackay in a dark alley, or big brooding Tommy Smith. With Nobby the toughness was only ever visible when he played. The rest of the time he was a lovely, likeable guy – his nickname was 'Happy' for a reason. Yet when Alf gave him a marking job to do he could tackle with the force of a rhinoceros. (Coincidentally, rhinos also have very poor eyesight.) It didn't seem to matter that, along with Bally, Nobby was the bantam-weight of the team. He certainly didn't look physically strong. There was just something about him. A lot of other players who were around the squad at the time could have fulfilled that role, but Nobby's attitude stood out and that was important to Alf.

I'm speculating here, but maybe it came from his upbringing. The fact that Nobby's father was an undertaker and he grew up around death must surely have toughened him up. He was also deeply affected by the Munich disaster that killed eight senior players. Several were Catholic like Nobby. He had been an altar boy growing up, and after the air crash in 1958 he served at the altar at requiem masses for men he'd looked up to. Nobby particularly worshipped Eddie Colman, a small nippy wing half who, aged just 21 and born a month after Duncan Edwards, was the tragedy's youngest victim. During his early years in the first team Nobby knew precisely how big were the boots that he had to fill, because he'd cleaned them many times as an apprentice.

So Alf's confidence in Nobby must have meant everything, and he felt it a duty to repay the debt. 'I would have died for him,' he said 40 years after the World Cup. 'He was such a man of his word. I could not see a single weakness in his approach as a manager. He treated you like an adult. He never hectored or laid down the law – and he was an Englishman through and through.'

By the time the World Cup came round, Alf had come to rely on the protection Nobby provided. Three games in, it was Nobby who needed Alf's protection. When we played France in our last group game, England required only a draw to qualify for the quarter-final. We won and got through but afterwards all the attention was on Nobby. In the middle of the park he came in from behind on the French midfielder Jacques Simon as he received a pass out of defence and turned in one move-ment. I was watching from the stands so didn't have the clearest view, but Simon's agony looked genuine enough and the grainy footage on YouTube suggests a case of GBH. George Cohen had a ringside seat. 'Jesus, that looked bad,' he remembered saying to himself. Nobby knew he'd got it horribly wrong and felt instant remorse. 'I couldn't go and say sorry to him,' he later said. 'That would have been hypocritical.'

Nobby had been booked earlier but, very luckily for him, this second foul was overlooked. After the game, the pundits piled into him on TV and then FIFA's official observer in the stand reported that, in his opinion, the referee had not done his job. The next day, FIFA issued a warning to the FA that 'if Stiles is reported to the committee again, either by a referee or official observer, serious action will be taken'.

Years later, Nobby could turn the whole incident into a joke.

'What did he do to deserve that?' he would say that George asked him.

'Called me Norbert.'

At the time, though, it was deadly serious. To put this in context, FIFA did an audit of foul play at the conclusion of the group stage. Pelé had been repeatedly mugged by opponents and limped out of the tournament. Three players would be sent off in the four quarter-finals. Nobby's confrontational style was in the spotlight. He wandered around the hotel with a long face, knowing that both the authorities and the media were trying to make an example of him. It was here that Alf stepped in. He thought it an outrage that FIFA seemed to be reffing games from the stands, and picking on Nobby. And he said so. He described it as 'a gross intimidation of a player'.

The quarter-final with Argentina was now bearing down on us, and Nobby was an obvious target for their dirty tricks. Alf needed players he could trust and so he grilled Nobby about the tackle. Was it a deliberate foul? 'I got my timing wrong, Alf,' said Nobby. 'I hate the fact I've put you in this position and all I can say is that I made a mistake. I went to make the tackle and then I found I was late – terribly late. I'm sorry.' Those might not have been Nobby's exact words, but that's how he remembered the exchange later. Whatever he said, it was good enough for Alf. Precisely how much pressure was really put on Alf to drop Nobby has never been fully revealed, but the day before the quarter-final the FA issued a statement: 'The sole responsibility for picking the England side rests in the hands of Mr Ramsey, as it has always done.' Nobby had been acquitted, or at least reprieved. It was a very emotional time for him. In the heat of the controversy he came close to tears when Alf went on TV to describe him as 'a great player'. As he prepared to go out against Argentina, Alf's two assistants both drummed it into Nobby that it was payback time. 'You'll never know what Alf has gone through for you,' Harold Shepherdson told him. In the dressing room, Les Cocker even pushed him against the wall and told him not to get into any trouble.

That's quite a threatening message to put into a player's head before such an important game. Nobby was brilliant against Argentina. He silenced the playmaker Ermindo Onega and, playing where he did and being who he was, he probably was the target of even more intimidation and gamesmanship than the rest of us. Not once did he flinch. It was such a dirty game that Nobby got a gag out of it that he'd use on the after-dinner speaking circuit. He imagined an exchange with the physio in the dressing room after the final whistle.

'Shep, come and take a look at this leg.'

'Why? What's wrong with it?'

'I don't know whose it is!'

Nobby wasn't just funny to look at. He could be a comedian too. He is always said to have come up with an even better line a few days later. Portugal loomed in the semi-final and Alf gave him the important task of marking Eusébio. 'Eusébio is capable of giving us a lot of problems,' Alf said to him, 'so I want you to take him out of the game.' 'Just for this game?' Nobby asked. 'Or for life?' Years later, Nobby couldn't remember whether he'd actually said this. He was sure that, if he did, it was a joke. I was in that team talk and I can't claim to remember it. But it certainly sounds like Nobby.

Either way, Nobby once again fulfilled his brief to the letter. The semi was probably the best game of the tournament, and the contest between Nobby and Portugal's star player was one of the great match-ups. They'd already met twice a few months earlier when Manchester United beat Benfica over two legs in the European Cup. Eusébio was now on a hot streak. He'd scored two against Brazil in the group, one of them a humdinger. Then in the quarter-final against North Korea he had dragged Portugal back from the dead, scoring four to get from 0–3 to 5–3. He knew England would not give him as much room and expressed his fears in the press. 'The referee must watch Stiles very, very carefully,' he said. 'He has been allowed to get away with too many things.'

When the biggest game of Eusébio's life came around, Nobby stuck to him like Velcro. Aside from the penalty he scored to make it 2–1 near the death, the great man barely had a sniff. He was a very good loser, going around shaking all our hands, but it clearly hurt and he left the pitch in tears.

It was unusual for Alf to single anyone out for special praise, but back in the dressing room he made an exception for Nobby and asked us to give him a round of applause. 'I had people helping me,' Nobby would modestly say. Unfortunately for him, he was the only one of us who couldn't celebrate that night. Alf permitted the squad two pints each but Nobby had to have an injection to stop him from developing cauliflower ear. He would have to proceed to the final fuelled by water and his own inner fire.

Bally's path through the World Cup was different from Nobby's. The rear six of Alf's team was firmly cemented in by the start of the tournament: Banksy and the back four with Nobby on patrol just in front. There was much more fluidity about the front five. Alf knew how to stop other teams getting on the scoresheet. That's why we didn't let in a single goal until eight minutes from the end of the semi with that Eusébio penalty. He was much less clear what the best formation was for scoring at the other end. Bally was one of Alf's options, but he had to go through hell to claim his place. In fact, he had to work far harder than any of us to become a footballer at all.

Bally was one of three members of the World Cup squad whose father had played professionally. George Eastham's dad played for Bolton, Blackpool and England. My father Charlie Hurst played at centre half for Bristol Rovers, Oldham and Rochdale, then for Chelmsford when we moved to Essex. I don't have strong memories of us talking much about football. What I do remember is the hours he spent with me working to improve my left-foot skills. I can still picture him in the back garden of our small council house, rolling the ball at me, patiently training muscle memory into my weaker foot. This would have been over a long period, because it wasn't something that could be taught on a couple of Sunday afternoons. I ask myself whether another father who wasn't an ex-footballer would have devoted so much time to teaching me that specific skill. Also, I wonder why he spent so long on it. It's not as if he ever leaned on me to follow him into the professional game. There was no talk of it at all. When I started to show promise in my teens, he certainly did nothing about it, so that's how come it was a friend of his who wrote off to Arsenal and West Ham asking them to offer me a trial.

Bally had the same left-foot training from his father. But he had so much more. His entire childhood was dominated by his

Judith didn't mind at all that the players' wives celebrated in a separate room at the Royal Garden Hotel in Kensington. Here she is with Tina Moore, her best friend Kathy Peters, Barbara Springett and Frances Bonetti.

The morning after, Judith and I have our picture taken reading the papers.

Judith cradling the man-of-the-match trophy I've just been awarded by the *News of the World*.

West Ham 4 West Germany 2. The two goalscorers with our captain.

Before the 1970 World Cup, the players were all offered use of a Ford Cortina. Mooro had a side hustle as a brown suede coat salesman.

Jimmy and I never talked about the World Cup final in any detail, not even when he joined me for a season at West Ham.

The 1966 team was reunited at the Café Royal for a testimonial dinner for Alf Ramsey after he was sacked as England manager in 1974.

With Claire, Joanne and Judith for my first trip to the Palace to collect an MBE in 1977.

Our beautiful, brave, exceptional daughter Claire.

The team minus the two Bobbys on a cruise. The extra men are the captain and Dave Watson of Sunderland and Man City.

The first of the golf days was in Surrey in 1998. I'm not sure where Banksy was that day.

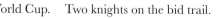

Judith gamely helping to bid for the 2006 World Cup.

Two knights on the bid trail.

In 2009, a wrong was righted and the rest of the squad were awarded World Cup winners medals by the Prime Minister Gordon Brown. George Cohen accepted Alf's on behalf of Lady Ramsey.

'The greatest player I've ever seen.' Jack presents his brother with the BBC Sports Personality of the Year Lifetime Achievement Award in 2008.

Hans Tilkowski and me in Baku in 2011 to mark a century of football in Azerbaijan in front of a statue of Tofiq Bahramov, who said the ball definitely crossed the line.

Among many reunions, this was a fun one with Banksy and Jimmy.

Near the 50th anniversary of 1966, Banksy, Ron Flowers, Roger Hunt, Bobby and I were guests in the Royal Box at Wimbledon.

In the end football didn't come home in 2021, but I did get to promote the Euros from the top of the London Eye.

Mooro, me, Bobby, Her Majesty and Roger.

dad's obsession with making a pro of him. Alan Ball Snr had played a bit for Southport then, long after my father was there, he too was on the books of Oldham and Rochdale. It doesn't seem to have been much of a career, so instead he loaded all his hopes onto his son. 'This boy will play for England,' he told one journalist. Bally was seven at the time!

The problem was that little Alan stayed little long into his teens. He grew to the same height and weight as Nobby. But even more than Nobby, he looked like a little scrap of a thing, and with that high voice of his he sounded like one too. Bolton, his home-town club where he went for trials, rejected him on grounds of size. So did Wolves.

But what Alan Ball Snr drummed into Alan Ball Jnr was determination. His whole childhood was devoted to improving his skills, his strength, his endurance, even his ability to receive a kick to the shin without flinching. Eventually Blackpool took him on. It was in training there that Bally came across Stanley Matthews, and vice versa. At 16, he released a pass for the great man, who was 30 years his senior, to run on to.

'When you play the ball to me, play it to my feet,' said Matthews.

'When I play it in front of you, get your fucking feet moving and get there,' replied Bally.

It's a funny story, and I've no doubt it's true. It tells you everything you need to know about Bally that he was prepared to be so rude to an elder statesman who first played for England long before Alan Jnr was a glint in Alan Snr's eye. The chasm in age and experience was that wide. What is interesting to me is what it says about the evolution of football. Sir Stanley, as he would become the year before the World Cup, was a footballer from the old school, a winger whose job was to dribble past the full back and cross from the byline. That's why he wanted the ball at his feet. He didn't want to have to fetch it. Bally was a brilliant dribbler too, but he was from the new breed of wide player who never ever stopped running: passes to run on to were what he lived for. And unlike the classic winger, he also tracked back to fetch and carry. He was a team player. Or at least he would become one.

In those early days, that self-belief could be his undoing. I found a revealing match report in my scrapbook from Bally's first years at Blackpool. 'Young Alan Ball is playing for the opposition and doesn't realise it. Ball tried to take on every man in sight in midfield, which brought no complaints from fast-covering West Ham.' It sounds as if he hadn't yet learned to play for the team.

Then there was his temper. When Bally got hot under the collar you could practically see the steam issuing from his ears. He was always getting booked in those days. It was almost inevitable that he'd get sent off too. It happened when he was playing for the Under 23s in 1965. In Vienna, only minutes after getting booked, he was whistled again and hurled the ball towards the referee in disgust. Off he went. He had only just won his first full cap, three days shy of his 20th birthday. It looks as if Alf decided to let him stew for a bit, because he didn't pick Bally again for another six months. He obviously learned his lesson. He came back for that epic win in Madrid, when England did without wings for the first time, and he played brilliantly.

Being exiled would have been terrible for Bally. Nothing got him quite so worked up as being left out. He always wanted to be in the thick of the action, and being left to cool his heels on the sideline was, for him, the ultimate frustration. I can still picture him chucking his boots against the wall in anger when he'd been left out of the team for one game. That was why, when we got to Lilleshall, he was more determined than anyone to make it into the final 22. He even kept an injury quiet so as not to miss a single session of training. 'I had to stay in that squad whatever it took,' he recalled. When Alf said he would announce the squad in alphabetical order, the name Ball came out first – ahead of Banks, Bonetti, Byrne, Charlton and Charlton. By his own admission, he was so relieved that he thought nothing for those who hadn't made the cut. But that was Bally: he was never not competing.

Like Nobby, he was totally devoted to Alf. That loyalty was established the first time he played for the Under 23s. It happened to be my first game at that level too, the one against Wales where Alf interrogated me on the train to Wrexham. Bally missed out on that ordeal because he was based in the north. 'Thank you for coming,' Alf said to him when they met. It was love at first sight. I think it was Alf's gentlemanliness that made such an impression on him. Bally had spent his entire life being driven on and on by his father, who was wary of praising him in case it softened him. Alf was much more caring. 'He wanted us to be a family,' Bally said of him. 'He wanted us to love each other. I remember him saying a general can't win wars and neither can foot soldiers but together they might.' He felt appreciated by Alf, and Alf in turn warmed to his passion. 'If you want my shirt back you are going to have to tear it off my back,' Bally once told him.

When the World Cup came around, Bally was duly selected to play in the first game against Uruguay. If you measure a match in corners gained, we battered them 15 to one. But it finished scoreless and Alf decided to shuffle his pack. In came Martin Peters and Terry Paine. Out went John Connelly and Alan Ball.

Obviously the mood in the room I shared with Martin was upbeat after that. It was a different story in the attic room occupied by Nobby and Bally. Bally was absolutely gutted. His whole life had been leading up to this moment and now he'd been cast out. I'm not saying he wandered around the hotel with a face like a slapped arse. That wouldn't be in his character. But with only Nobby for a witness, he vented his rage and hurt as only he could. He was a great one for betting on the nags, and he'd just had a success. Always down the bookies, on this occasion he came back with 50 quid in used fivers. 'Fuck Ramsey,' he sang repeatedly as he tossed the notes on the floor.

The two of them found a way to keep each other buoyant. Nobby saw Bally through his brief period of exile from the team, and when Nobby was in the crosshairs after that foul on Simon, it was Bally's turn to keep his morale up. This probably became easier once he knew he'd been recalled ahead of the quarter-final.

Bally's joy at being back in the side found its fullest expression in the way he celebrated my goal. No sooner had I glanced my header across the Argentine keeper than Bally pounced on me and leapt into my arms like a date at a high-school prom. We were only just emerging from the handshake era in 1966.

Players were still learning to be effusive and tactile. Bally's displays of emotion helped change all that. Mind you, I don't suppose he'd have done it to Sir Stanley Matthews.

The day before the final, we had a putting tournament at Roehampton, which Bally won. Then that night Alf led us to the cinema in Hendon. *Those Magnificent Men in Their Flying Machines* was showing. In other words, a film about achieving aerial dominance over the Germans. Was this subliminal messaging, or just a nice change from yet another western? Afterwards, Bally recalled that 'nobody left the picture house. They just stood and clapped us. We were ordinary lads. We were going to win the World Cup for them tomorrow.' The odd thing is that, at that point, Bally had no idea if he'd be on the pitch. The rest of us already knew – Alf had had a quiet word that evening. He didn't tell Bally till the next morning.

Over the years, whenever the team got together, we'd sometimes throw around various theories about what Alf was thinking. Was he waiting on Jimmy Greaves? Was Bally going to be the one who was sacrificed to make room for him? I doubt it. Alf had found his winning team and he wasn't going to change it. To me it seems much more likely that Alf wanted to keep his little fireball aflame with desire for as long as possible. So he let him simmer and stew overnight. 'I'm keeping the same team that beat the Portuguese,' Alf told him at breakfast. 'You'll play the right side of Bobby Charlton. Congratulations, have a fantastic day.'

And he did, and so did Nobby.

14
CLAIRE

F rom the outside it must look like a wonderful way to live. You do a job you love and thousands of people turn up every week to cheer you at your work. But success on the football pitch is no defence against the difficulties of life, and many of my teammates and I suffered our share of tragedy.

For Bobby Charlton and Nobby Stiles, there was the life-changing trauma of the Munich air disaster. Jimmy Greaves endured the loss of a baby son at less than six months. Gordon Banks's disabled older brother was beaten up and died of his injuries in hospital. George Cohen's mother was killed by a lorry. In 2000, several of us from the 1966 team were on a Mediterranean cruise when George received news that his brother Peter (father of the England rugby player Ben Cohen), who ran a night club in Northampton, had died in hospital a month after trying to break up a fight in his club. Peter lived with the pain of seeing the three men who were arrested following the assault acquitted of manslaughter.

Grief entered my life in 1974 when my younger brother Robert committed suicide. He was 28.

It's a very long time ago. As I was preparing to tell the story of this chapter, my sister Diane texted a reminder on the day it would have been our brother's 78th birthday. I have to confess that his suicide remains a mystery to me. I was four years older than Robert and, by my mid-teens, I was not spending a lot of time with him. My life was taken up by football in the winter, cricket in the summer, and then I left Chelmsford at 17 to go and live in digs in east London as a West Ham apprentice. Soon Judith and I were together, so my focus was elsewhere. By the time I became a first-team regular, Rob would have been leaving school and all I can remember of visits to my parents is that he was almost never there.

So what went wrong? He was also good at football and cricket but seemed to lack my knack for application and discipline. He found it hard to hold down work and had a difficult relationship with a girlfriend whose parents didn't want Rob anywhere near her. Clearly there were problems with mental health. The fact that I was ignorant of his troubles is partly down to the culture of the family we both grew up in. We weren't very demonstrative and, typically for the period, we weren't encouraged to discuss our feelings. For me, the gulf deepened with my parents' gradual withdrawal from my life after the World Cup. Then there is the wider ignorance of mental health issues, which were much less discussed and understood in the 1960s.

It could be that my memory has erased the details of Rob's struggles, but when I ask Judith what she can remember of that time, she also draws a blank. 'He was such a handsome, lovely boy,' she says. 'I think he was in his own little world.' Two of our daughters were born while Rob was still alive, and we don't think he saw either of them very much. This is not because we avoided contact with him. He simply stayed away. I've always been led to believe that he was not affected by my professional success. Quite the contrary. Not many years ago, I was grateful to receive a touching letter from someone who had served time with Rob in a young offenders institution. My brother was in there for doing something wild and silly rather than genuinely criminal. Their sentences found them inside in the summer of 1966. They watched the World Cup final together and he wrote to me to share his memory of that day:

> We sat together on wooden fold-up chairs and had to threaten a riot to watch extra time. Rob must have jumped four feet in the air every time you scored. He was very very proud of you. We shared many jokes together in difficult circumstances. I was grateful to find a good friend in such harsh conditions.

In 1972 we moved to Stoke, so I was insulated from the troubles in my parents' marriage. My mother's decision to leave my father seemed to have an impact on Rob. In 1974 he fetched up in a psychiatric unit. Soon after he was released, he threw himself under a train at Chelmsford station.

Aside from the huge shock that anyone would experience at such news, I remember a feeling of total surprise. I had an idea that things were not right with Rob. But whatever I knew about his issues, I never for a moment imagined during all that period that he was likely to commit suicide. I simply couldn't believe it. The club gave me compassionate leave for a month while I tried to come to terms with this dreadful and sudden loss. It could be argued that I never really have. My parents got divorced the following year and the family I had grown up in officially no longer existed.

Several years later I was working for Anglia TV when I was visited by a memory of Rob. This must have been the early 1980s. Every Saturday I would go to a game in East Anglia and then head on Sunday to the studio in Norwich to talk about it on regional television. Mostly I drove but one Sunday I went by train. Maybe it wasn't long after the icy night one winter around that time when my Cortina slid off the road into a field, doing a couple of rolls on the way. That day on the train I remember sitting in one of those old-fashioned compartments with six seats in a largely empty carriage when the guard came in to check my ticket. He apologised about the lack of a buffet or catering trolley and kindly offered to make me a cup of tea. When he came back with the mug, he lingered as if there was something he wanted to get off his chest. And he told me that he had been working on the train that killed my brother. I don't know which one of us was more affected by the memory. While he felt for me, I felt for him.

The consolation after Robert's death was that I had my own growing family. Judith and I became parents at the same time as a ridiculous number of my West Ham teammates. Several of us having married at the same time, the inevitable happened. There were so many young dads in 1965 that a local paper did a news story. Shooting us from overhead, the photographer lined us all up as if we were in our positions on a pitch, although there were 12 fathers in the squad cradling their children. (Technically, Johnny Byrne's baby arrived in 1964.) Martin Peters held up Lee Ann and Bobby Moore was with little Roberta. Claire and I were at the front. In a second photo we were joined by the mothers. When Judith looks at the cutting now she's annoyed to see she was caught smoking a cigarette.

There was a redhead gene in the Harries family. When Claire arrived on 30 October 1965 it was clear she had inherited it. She was a very good baby and, after Joanne was born four years later, a very good sister. We love remembering the innocent things that came out of her mouth in those early years. Claire didn't entirely understand the words she was taught to say at the Catholic primary school we sent her to in our part of east London.

'We said "Hail Mary" today,' she'd tell us. 'Hail Mary, full of grace, blessed are diamonds and swimming.'

'I don't think it's that,' her mum would say.

'I've got an encloptia,' she'd reply.

One day she discovered a new word.

'Do you know, Mummy, what some people say when they blow off? They say fart.'

'I've never heard that before,' Judith replied, playing along. 'How do you spell that?'

'P. H. A. U. G. H. T.'

She did very well at school. The only cloud we remember from her early life is the day someone said something to her about having a famous father. It so happened that she went to school with Roberta Moore, so she wasn't the only child making a discovery that set her slightly apart. This is something that all our girls would struggle with as it made them feel singled out. Joanne and Charlotte still do. They get embarrassed if it's pointed out. They've always wanted to be accepted for who they are, rather than for who their father is.

Claire was a very gentle and ladylike child, but she had a sting in her tail and could stand up for herself when she felt like it. Judith remembers the time she took Claire to have her eyes tested and it turned out she needed to wear glasses. She said, 'I'm not wearing glasses.' The optician calmly told her that she really needed to. She held up her hand and repeated, 'I am *not* wearing glasses.' She was about ten at the time.

She needed that strength of character to cope with all the moving. When a footballer gets a transfer from one club to another, all the media and the fans think of is the impact he might have on the pitch. Will he be missed at his old club? Will he be any good at his new club? But the player doesn't just uproot his own life. His family comes with him, and they have a lot of adapting to do too. Claire was eight when we moved to Stoke, 13 when we returned south and 16 when I got a job in Kuwait. She just dealt with it, and each time did her best to fit into her new surroundings.

The one time we worried about her was when she started at a Catholic secondary school in Surrey where she was horribly bullied by a group of girls. Judith went in to see the mother superior, and got a feeble response. 'I think you should phone the parents,' she said. 'That's not my job,' Judith replied. 'That's yours.' Years later Claire happened to spot her bullies in the street and reported back to her mother. 'Mum,' she said, 'if you saw these girls at the station, you'd see I've come out on top.'

I mention these experiences because to some extent they must have fireproofed her for the ordeal to come. Claire continued her schooling in Kuwait with us. By then the subjects she excelled at were French and Spanish, but because it was difficult to study them in Kuwait, her private French teacher thought she ought to try university in France. So from 17 she spent two years at the Université d'Angers. By the time she finished we were back in Surrey and she started working in London, first as a receptionist in a hotel, then as a PA in Bond Street.

In her early twenties, Claire fell in love, got married and at 22 was expecting her first child. She was 20 weeks pregnant when one day she phoned her mother from work and Judith could not understand a word she was saying. The words coming out of her mouth were gobbledygook. Someone at the other end came on the phone and explained that Claire was not well.

Claire would later describe the symptoms herself.

> Without any warning, I opened my mouth to talk and all that came out was unintelligible nonsense. Overnight my brain had stopped me from constructing words. It merely allowed me to release a series of noises, with no on–off button; my mouth would literally run away with itself, and I was powerless to stop it. My right hand was also flinching, moving spasmodically when it felt like it.

That evening she came home to us and we saw for ourselves that something was wrong. It was extremely worrying. We took her to our doctor that night. He required us to leave the room in order that, in private, he could ask Claire if she was a member of a religious cult. He seemed to think she was speaking in tongues. This was the first and most extreme proof that the medical profession had absolutely no idea what was wrong with her.

She was eventually prescribed a drug to lower her heart rate. In the meantime, she gave birth to Amy. The symptoms went away for a while. Whenever they returned she would have what she called one of her 'dos'. She learned how to manage it somewhat by simply avoiding speech. We got used to listening to her and teasing out what she was trying to say. Doctors would dismiss her symptoms as a manifestation of stress. This seemed crazy when the main cause of her stress and occasional anxiety attacks was obviously the fear that she was going to have another episode. It was only when she had one in front of a new GP that someone from the medical profession at last saw first-hand that something was wrong. Claire was expecting her second child when a neurologist diagnosed epilepsy – wrongly, as it turned out.

She lived with her condition for several years before we could get an accurate diagnosis. It wasn't until I happened to be in Harley Street and bumped into Dr Adrian Whiteson, who worked for the British Boxing Board of Control, that something shifted. He suggested Claire have a scan. So we took her to see Professor Lindsay Symon at the National Hospital for Neurology and Neurosurgery in central London, and that's when we discovered that she had a glioma, a slow-growing brain tumour.

She really felt comfortable with Professor Symon. After all the worry of not knowing what was wrong with her, here was someone who was calm and exuded authority. The only problem was that he was due to retire. He explained the options. 'We can leave it a while or we can operate,' he said. If she was going to have an operation, Claire wanted him to do it.

When she went in for surgery for the first time to treat a grade 3 oligodendroglioma, she showed the mettle that would be with her through thick and thin. 'Where are you?' they asked as she started to come round from the anaesthetic. 'Butlin's holiday camp,' she replied. We'd decided that I should go to work and Judith to the hospital. That changed when Claire saw her mother's face and said, 'Where's Dad?' Judith called me at work and I came into London as fast as I could.

This was in 1995. Claire had six weeks of radiotherapy at the Royal Marsden. She lost her hair and tried various hairpieces that all looked like birds' nests. Eventually we had a hairpiece made for her and the manufacturer got famous hair stylist Nicky Clarke to fit it for a photoshoot. 'Typical,' she said. 'I had to lose my hair to get an appointment with Nicky Clarke.' Two or three times, we took her to Paris to receive hair transplants.

For a number of years her symptoms were in abeyance and she was able to get on with her life. By now, she was working part-time as a PA for a vicar in Cobham. They got on well and we only learned many years later that she had confided in him. 'I have a really hard fight on my hands,' she told him. 'I want to live till my children reach their twenties.'

There were many happy times. The proudest day of my life came in 1998 when Judith, Claire, Joanne and Charlotte accompanied me to Buckingham Palace on the day I received a knighthood. In the photo of the five of us taken by Monte Fresco outside the Palace, Claire looks a wonderful picture of health. Her optician would have been pleased to see she'd finally agreed to wear glasses.

A couple of years later her marriage came to an end and the family started piece by piece to move to Cheltenham.

Claire arrived with her son Jack a year after us. She was never quite a single mother because I was now officially retired and so Judith and I were both free to take on some of the childcare responsibilities. But she never allowed ill health to stop her from being a very competent mother, while also getting a job with a charity.

We now feel that the move to Cheltenham was meant to be. From Surrey we'd make trips into London for appointments at the Royal Marsden, where we all felt they didn't know Claire from Adam. In Cheltenham, her home was five minutes from what turned out to be a very good oncology department.

This mattered because in 2004 things suddenly changed for the worse soon after she spotted that her right leg was starting to drag and she felt abnormal sensation in her right hand. She wrote:

> I deteriorated very quickly, almost overnight. I had a scan on 18 October and by 4 November I was having surgery, once again thankfully successfully. However, my tumour had changed its spots to become a glioblastoma, a more serious, cancerous tumour and more unpredictable.

The surgical procedure known as debulking removed some of the tumour as it grew. In 2005 she was put on a complex round of medication and started on a brutal course of chemotherapy that went on in various forms for years. When people asked Claire how she'd lost weight, she'd explain with a straight face that she was on the chemo diet.

She used these years to make an impact. When a Maggie's Centre was opened in Cheltenham by the Duchess of Cornwall, Claire was invited to attend. She was seen as such a model patient that her oncologists asked her to phone up other patients and reassure them when they had received the same diagnosis. Dr Sean Elyan, her new oncologist, was so impressed by the way she understood her situation and her treatment that in 2007 she was commissioned to write a piece about her tumour for *Target*, the magazine of Brain Tumour UK. You can tell from the way she wrote that she refused to let herself give way to despair.

> All in all, I've been very lucky. My children are teen-agers now and becoming more independent; so I can start having more 'me' time with reflexology, acupuncture and aromatherapy massage, along with my daily walking, which I love. I have been living with a brain tumour for nearly 20 years and I live virtually the same life as I would be living if I did not have cancer and I am grateful for that.

Over these years there were three debulking operations, though these could go only so far because otherwise they would have affected Claire's movement. She thought very highly of her neurosurgeon Mr George Malcolm, who saw her at the Frenchay Hospital in Bristol. They got to know each other so well that she developed a shorthand for whenever she thought his medical explanations were going into too much detail. She would just put up her hand and he'd keep it brief.

The surgical interventions seemed to come along in a never-ending cycle. For one of the more dramatic operations she had a bleed where they had to remove the top of her skull. She was in hospital for seven weeks then, and for a while she had to wear a protective helmet. 'Look what they've done to me now,' she said to a friend.

Her cancer and the treatment became part of the rhythm of our lives. 'The physical and psychological trauma of this treatment clearly necessitates strong support from her family,' wrote Dr Elyan in one set of medical notes. That was in 2008, when Claire came with us on a summer holiday to Barbados. She enjoyed herself but it was noticeable how tired she was throughout.

How long she would have was something none of us knew. She wouldn't voice the thought often, because that's not necessarily what you talk about when living with cancer long term. I do remember once driving her to a medical appointment. As she got out of the car she said to me, 'I've got a ticking time bomb in my head, Dad.' You don't want to react too negatively when your daughter says something like that. Your role is to be the support, the pillar she can lean on, and to show no signs of crumbling. Inside I felt as if I was being crucified.

After one appointment in Bristol, we got on the phone to Judith, who asked how it had gone. 'Oh yeah, fine,' said Claire. But Judith knew.

By now Claire's mobility had deteriorated and she had to use a wheelchair. Then the tumour was found to have spread into the base of her neck. We were told this was unusual. It was only at this very late stage that Claire at last flared into anger. 'This is a fucking bastard,' she said to her oncologist. 'You're right,' agreed Dr Elyan. 'It *is* a fucking bastard.' Claire never swore. It's a sign of how in tune they were that he broke with medical convention and used the same language.

Looking back at the correspondence in her medical notes, I see that by early 2009 it was reported that Claire:

> … understands that she has incurable recurrence of her malignancy and that the aim of treatment is to try and optimise control of her symptoms, and survival … She is definitely keen to consider experimental options and her father (Sir Geoff Hurst, footballer) is equally, if not more, keen to consider such options.

We were clinging to the hope that there was a miracle at the end of the rainbow. I took her to see a professor in Switzerland. We went to a meeting where a doctor from Johns Hopkins Hospital in Baltimore promised the earth. 'It's up to you, Claire,' said her oncologist, 'but I don't think it's going to work.'

Still we held back from saying anything out of that instinct to protect her. 'You always make me feel there's nothing wrong,' Claire once said to us. Judith did her best to pretend that everything was normal, even if Claire sat at the table having a fit. But there was no hiding from the reality that our gracious, classy daughter, who was so admired by all our male friends, was now desperately ill. Judith admits that sometimes she wished for Claire's sake it could be over.

By the autumn of 2010 she needed to be looked after, so a hospital bed was delivered and she moved in with us. Help was offered but it didn't arrive so at nights Judith found herself having to lift her much taller daughter. A few days later, Dr Elyan paid a surprise visit. 'If it was me,' he told Judith, 'I would want to go to the hospice. They're not always easy to get into, but you've got to start being her mother now and not her carer.' Then he walked into Claire's room. She'd never seen him anywhere but an oncology department before. 'What are you doing here?' she said.

We were worried that Claire might dig her heels in and so we deputed Jack to ask her whether she wanted to go to a hospice. By now, Jack was an adult who had lived with the knowledge of his mother's illness for all of his 20 years. They had a very trusting relationship – he would be the one she chose to shave her head. When he broached the subject of the hospice she just said, 'Hallelujah.'

The thought of sending your child into a hospice is genuinely horrendous. Claire had been to hospices for respite care, but this wasn't that. 'You know I'm going to end up in there one day,' she once said after a massage. The day they came to pick her up was stressful enough. The ambulance staff would have known that they had come to collect a dying woman but one of them couldn't stop himself. 'Oh, it's Geoff Hurst,' he said as he came into the flat. If I shrugged, Judith seethed. Once at the hospice, one of the nurses couldn't handle the fact that I was in their midst. In the end, we had to contrive a way to get him out of the room.

Mostly, for those two weeks Claire was cared for by a wonderful male nurse. Overall, the experience could not have been more peaceful, for her or for us. We were able to be with her 24/7. The family all came. Her children Amy and Jack, her sisters, Judith's sisters who flew over from America. Judith slept in the room with her while her sisters slept in the lounge outside. Towards the end, Claire was not eating and not really speaking, and we don't know how aware she was of her surroundings or even if she could hear us.

In a sense she was already gone. And then eventually she was. She was 45.

George Malcolm, speaking at Claire's funeral, described us as a stoical family. If that's true, we took our lead from our daughter. In a letter to us, Sean Elyan expressed the wish that 'her indomitable spirit' could somehow be bottled. 'It is extremely rare to feel inspired by patients,' he wrote. 'I can honestly say that I lost count of the number of times I experienced this feeling with Claire.' He praised her determination to take on even the most unpleasant treatments, and her relentless refusal to complain, and her smile. 'We sometimes reflect as doctors on "a patient I will never forget",' he concluded. 'I need to pay no greater tribute than to tell you all that for me that person was Claire.'

We received condolences from medical professionals and from friends, including all my old teammates. The next golf day was very emotional.

As for me, I still find the thought of visiting Claire's grave too painful to contemplate. For years, I found it difficult if not impossible even to talk about her loss. If people asked I would just say, 'I've got three daughters.' It was easier not to have to explain that one of them was no longer with us. 'When you lose a child you have a life before and you have a life after,' says Judith. 'It's not the same. You never get over it. Ever.'

We talk about her, and laugh about the times we had with her. Her quirk of driving the wrong way through a 'No Entry' sign in Cheltenham. The evening she went to an Italian restaurant and got so annoyed with the rude service that she stuffed one of those outsize peppermills in her coat and walked off with it. The time she misheard the wording of the 'Hail Mary'. 'Hail Mary, full of grace, blessed are diamonds and swimming.'

Hers is not the sort of story you expect to read in the middle of a book about football and footballers. But having struggled for years to talk about her life and her death, here I am – with Judith – remembering her. Our beautiful, brave, exceptional daughter, Claire.

15

HUNT AND GREAVSIE

N ot that long ago my wife and I were boarding a plane. Judith took the window seat and I parked myself in the middle. At a certain point a man arrived to occupy the aisle seat. I must have said something to him, which opened the conversation, because no sooner had he looked at my face than he told me he happened to live just ten minutes from me in Cheltenham, and that he was a Liverpool fan.

Obviously, I thought to myself, *he knows who I am.*

Only he didn't, quite.

'You're Roger Hunt, aren't you?' he said.

'As you're a Liverpool fan,' I replied as diplomatically as I could, 'you'll know that Roger passed away a few years ago.'

Then I got up to go to the toilet. When I came back, I found him leaning across my vacant seat and talking to my wife.

'Did you tell him?' I said to Judith so only she could hear.

'No,' she replied. 'He worked it out for himself.'

Nobody, on the other hand, ever mistook me for Jimmy Greaves.

Tall tales starring Jimmy could fill a whole book. In fact, he filled several books with them himself. One of my favourite stories concerns the occasion – which I have mentioned in 'Sweet FA' – when he, Banksy and I were guests at Wembley in 2014. The World Cup trophy was being taken on a tour of every nation participating in that year's tournament. It was flown around the globe by a couple of FIFA reps. One of them was wearing white gloves and I asked him why.

'The only people that can hold the trophy without white gloves,' he explained, 'are the team that have won it.'

Jimmy piped up.

'That poses a very important question,' he said in that slow, twinkling drawl of his. 'If it gets nicked there's only my fucking fingerprints on it.'

Much to the embarrassment of the FA, the Jules Rimet trophy was notoriously nicked in 1966, and then found again by a black and white collie called Pickles. I duly got my fingerprints on it, while Jimmy Greaves never did. In the eyes of the public, of fans who know their English football history, that fact came to define both of us.

How it happened was that sliding-doors moment, which lasted no longer than an instant, when the studs of a Frenchman gashed Jimmy's left shin to the bone in the third group game. He played on for the rest of the match, not realising anything was badly wrong, then pulled off his boot in the dressing room to find it full of blood. It meant he was out and I was in, which is where I stayed.

But is there more to the story than blind chance? What really happened to put my name into the World Cup's record books and keep his out of it?

There's many a game of what-if that can be played about the 1966 tournament. In football, as in cards or with dice, luck plays a big part in determining outcomes. Take those letters my father's friend sent off asking two London clubs to give me a trial when I was a teenager. What if I'd been apprenticed not to West Ham but to Arsenal? Without Ron Greenwood guiding my early career, I might have stayed a wing half all my life. I'd certainly never have done those 10,000 hours of near-post heading practice. So I wouldn't have had the telepathic connection with Martin Peters and Bobby Moore, which led to my winner in the quarter-final and my equaliser in the final. Or what if, in the pre-tournament warm-up tour, I'd not been knackered by heavy training the day before playing Denmark and had been able to give a better account of myself? Maybe then I'd have been in the World Cup team from the start, and if it had been me who hadn't scored in the group games it could have been me who was dropped before the knockout stage.

Now for Jimmy. What if he hadn't contracted hepatitis in the autumn of 1965? The illness cost him three months of the season and lost him half a yard of pace that he said never returned. Otherwise he'd have surely slotted in a couple of goals in the group games and I'd have stayed in the stands for the whole tournament. What if Jimmy wore shinpads? He didn't like them because he said they took the edge off his explosive burst of speed. If he'd had some on he'd not have been injured by a French midfielder. Then Alf would have had a different decision to make before the quarter-final. To stick or to twist? Could Alf really have been brave or ruthless enough to leave out his star striker? Here was a genius who had been scoring goals for fun all his life. His four against Norway on that warm-up tour took his England tally to 43 in 49, including six hattricks. Six! That's still a record, one up from Lineker and (at the time of writing) from Kane, and in far fewer games. How could anyone drop such a colossus and instead draft in a rookie with only five caps and a solitary goal – and who was crap against Denmark?

Also, what if there had been subs? What then? Might Alf have risked Jimmy and brought me on if needed? Or the other way round?

Only one thing is certain in this maze of permutations. Once the tournament got underway, Alf was never going to do without the services of Roger Hunt.

People must look at our World Cup squad for 1966 and gawp at its imbalance. But there's a logic to Alf's choice. In those days there was much less positional fluidity. Stoppers were there to stop strikers. Full backs were there to stop wingers. As for wingers, they were there to beat full backs. And Alf picked three of them: Connelly, Paine, Callaghan. It now looks like over-indulgence. It's as if he couldn't bear to go into the tournament without that magic DNA to call on. He must have hoped that one of them might turn out to be the next Finney or another Matthews. They didn't. So after three games he threw up his hands and changed tack. Not just for the World Cup. Forever. John Connelly and Terry Paine never played for England again, while Cally had to wait till 1977, when he was in his mid-thirties and Ron Greenwood was in charge, to get his next cap.

But what if Alf had picked only two wingers? That would have created room for four strikers. I'd have had to budge up and make room for a rival. So I guess I was the ultimate benefi-ciary. When Jimmy's shin was kicked, there was only me waiting in the stands. Not me and A.N. Other.

In retrospect, I can see that relying on only three strikers might look daft. It was perhaps less so back then. Because there were no substitutes, it's not as if Alf had the option of loading the bench with alternatives in case one striker had an off day. So he plumped for three, and made sure that each of them could give him something different.

Greaves. Hunt. Hurst.

Cavalry. Infantry. Artillery.

Poacher. Grafter. Bruiser.

But who would he play? It was always going to be two from three. Alf would never at any point have considered throwing on all three front players. But I think he was uncertain which two to go with. Looking back at the games England played when I first came into the side in February, I see that I was up front with Roger in one match and then in the next with Jimmy, who was coming back from his illness. While Alf hadn't made his mind up, I did seem to be the one fixed point. After Lilleshall, the 22 was announced and the squad numbers were assigned. These implied that I was in Alf's thoughts for the first team. If the numbers meant anything, up front it was going to be Jimmy, number 8, and me, number 10. Roger later admitted that being given the number 21 made him draw the same conclusion.

Then we flew off on the four-game tour. I didn't score for three games, had my shocker against Denmark and got dropped. In the last warm-up match, against Poland in Chorzow, Roger spectacularly drove home the only goal. It was his 11th in only his 12th cap. So his strike rate and Jimmy's were both up at nearly one a game. A phenomenal record. Mine was one every five. As a result, although they'd played only three matches together – the same number of times I'd played with Roger – it was no surprise to me that for the three group games it was Hunt and Greaves out there wearing 8 and 21 while the number 10 shirt stayed in the kitman's bag.

I was absolutely not disappointed by Alf's choice. Roger and Jimmy were two of the great strikers of the 1960s and I'd played just a couple of games. Never having expected to play for England at all, I was delighted to be there in any capacity. So while I was watching, I wasn't waiting.

Then Jimmy has his disaster.

I remember the first time I saw Jimmy at close quarters. He was between clubs, having secured a big transfer from Chelsea to AC Milan in the summer of 1961. He was already a star in his very early twenties, and blimey he could do things with a football. I was still a wing half in my late teens and my eyes were out on stalks. He stayed only a few months in Italy, soon moving to Spurs, where I now started to play against him for West Ham. In those years I may have seen him out with Bobby Moore. They had become close friends and a kind of double act, Mooro as straight man to Jimmy with his wicked sense of humour. Jimmy used to tell a great story about how the two of them bonded when England went to Chile for the 1962 World Cup. Before the tournament the squad stayed in a remote mining village in the Andes. The pair of them were billeted together in a shack with a corrugated iron roof where they would lie awake listening to every reverberating raindrop. By the time they reached the quarter-final they couldn't wait to get home to east London. 'We were very lonely,' said Jimmy. 'I think all the team was. When we got knocked out against Brazil, Vavá scored the third goal and we all

ran up and congratulated him because then we could go home.'
(In fact, Garrincha was the scorer.)

I knew him much less well than Mooro did, so the day I bumped into Jimmy in Romford High Street sticks out. This encounter can be precisely dated to late 1965, when he was recovering from hepatitis and I was about to be selected for England for the first time. I know this because my daughter Claire was a tiny baby of only two months and I was pushing her in her pram. Jimmy was in a tobacconist stocking up on supplies for his pipe, which was an unusual habit for a footballer even then. The players who smoked, like Jack and Mooro, stuck to cigarettes. I was chuffed to see him so I pushed Claire in for a chat. Possibly it was the first proper one-to-one conversation I'd ever had with him, and I was hypnotised by his charisma. So hypnotised that when we left the shop and went our separate ways, I looked around me in the street and realised I'd completely forgotten I was a new dad and had left little Claire in the tobacconist's.

A few months later, at Lilleshall, I had more prolonged exposure. What stood out was his wit, his intelligence and his irreverent approach to authority. Later in the decade he had more of a cooling off with Alf, but for now you could just tell that he didn't take the bosses, either Alf or his sidekicks, as seriously as they might have wished. Did this tell against him later on in the tournament when Alf came to select the team for the final? I genuinely have no idea. All I know is that he was brilliant at the job he did.

He was still working hard to recover his strength after the hepatitis. On the training pitch I was left in no doubt that he was a great athlete. Using the power in well-developed thighs, and a low centre of gravity, he could sprint and twist with incredible dexterity. I don't suppose he'd have finished on the podium in a 100-yard dash, but he didn't need to be quick over distance. He needed speed over five or ten yards. And he didn't have to be as fit as either Roger or me. Our style of play was built on running our markers into the ground, pulling them around the pitch and wearing them down through sheer energy. The way Jimmy played, he wouldn't have to work as hard as lesser talents to gain some kind of advantage because he had the skill to be in the right place at the right time. He had incredible anticipation, and a sixth sense for space. There might be close to 20 players crowding in and around the penalty area, and somehow he'd be standing there almost on his own. Or he could dribble his way into space, like someone picking a lock to slip into an empty room. And when he got a shot in, there was none of that blowing the bloody doors off. Jimmy's signature wasn't the bulging net, the thumped drive that in freezeframe looks like he's clearing a high hurdle. No, he'd caress the ball in, as if he was crown green bowling. Scoring for him was almost intellectual. It was about solving riddles.

I firmly believe that Jimmy Greaves was the greatest goal-scorer ever to have played for England. It's because of this that I struggle to accept the idea that he wouldn't have played in the final if fit. For me, if he'd recovered from his shin injury, he would have been on that pitch. This is not me being modest. For Alf to leave him out would have been one of the biggest risks any football manager could take.

Whether it's a good thing that he didn't play is for others to say, not me. There's an argument that Jimmy fared better when paired with bigger strike partners, as he always was at Spurs, and that I'd have been a better fit for him than Roger. You could equally say that without substitutes it would have been foolish to send him on only ten days after having 14 stitches.

'How's your mate?' Alf asked Mooro during Jimmy's desperate days in the treatment room. 'He seems very quiet.' No doubt Mooro heard things from his teammate that were for no one else's ears, but he was always discreet and he could only shrug in reply. On the day of the semi-final there was a training session for the reserves at London Colney, the Arsenal training ground, which was much closer to the hotel than Roehampton. I notice from the photos of the day that Jimmy wore shinpads. By the time the final came round three days later, a report in my scrapbook tells me that he had declared himself fit. In a cricket match at Roehampton he had a bowl and got Nobby Stiles out, caught by Bobby Charlton. When we talked about it in the privacy of our room, Martin and I certainly assumed he'd be playing. The *Evening Standard* hedged its bets. On the morning of the match it listed Jimmy among 12 England player profiles under the headline, THE MEN WHO MEET IN TODAY'S FINAL.

The fact that I played and Jimmy didn't is not something we ever talked about in any depth. This is not because I felt any guilt. I didn't, not even for a second. That's the sport we were in. There are injuries and there are suspensions, and if one player can't be on the pitch the player who comes in can't be expected just to keep the seat warm for him. We both knew this.

On the night of the final Jimmy slipped away, ducking out of the official celebration at the Royal Garden Hotel to go on holiday to Majorca with his family. 'A touch of the Greta

Garbos,' he later called it. He returned to the England team the following season, but eventually asked Alf not to pick him unless intending to play him. His next appearance at a World Cup was in an unofficial capacity. He and a co-driver took part in a World Cup rally starting at Wembley, which passed through 25 countries in Europe and South America, ending up 16,000 miles later at the Azteca Stadium. The epic trip even sent him back to the Andes. When he finally drove his Ford Escort into Mexico City, he dropped in on Mooro, who had been sprung from house arrest in Colombia after the infamous saga of the Bogotá bracelet and was being hosted in a British embassy residence. Jimmy had to clamber over a wall to get in. He loved retelling this story with a bit of top spin. He'd say the embassy he broke into was in Bogotá. 'It's a good job Bobby gave me the bracelet as I was leaving,' Jimmy would say, 'otherwise he would have been right in the shit.'

By 1970 the three of us were all teammates at West Ham. Jimmy had come from Spurs in a part-exchange which saw Martin go in the other direction. So Mooro and I had waved goodbye to one friend but said hello to another. One of my favourite photos from my time at West Ham is of Jimmy and me at Chadwell Heath, arm in arm and both wearing broad smiles. For one season, I had the qualified pleasure of playing up front with him. It was qualified because actually he took part in only 16 matches in total. By then, he clearly wasn't happy with his game or fully fit and was starting to depend on alcohol. At the end of the season he retired. He was only 31.

In later life, the only evidence left on Jimmy's body of a bruising career in football was the scar on his shin from the wound inflicted by the French midfielder. Did watching England win the World Cup without him leave an internal scar? People read a lot into the press photos of him on the England bench in extra time, unsmiling and seeming not to join in the celebrations. In a BBC interview with the sports journalist Ian Wooldridge recorded in 1982, he had the courage and honesty to admit he felt like 'the loneliest man in Wembley Stadium that particular day'. He explained to Wooldridge how he had always had faith in England's ability to win the World Cup, but took it for granted that his contribution would be a key ingredient in the triumph. 'What I never ever thought was that we would win it and I wouldn't be in the side, that I wouldn't actually be on that field in the final. And it was a tremendous blow to me.'

It's often been suggested that he used alcohol to obliterate the pain of missing out. I couldn't say for sure, but my agent and great friend Terry Baker came to know Jimmy incredibly well in the last 20 years of his life and is adamant that it's not the case. According to Terry, 1966 haunted him only because no one would shut up about it. 'I know a lot of people think I became an alcoholic after missing a World Cup final,' Jimmy said. 'But when you've lost a son at six months old, whatever anyone thinks missing an effing game of football doesn't matter a toss.'

Amen to that.

One thing I know for certain is Jimmy would hate to think that, in all this talk of Greaves v. Hurst, the limelight had been stolen from Hunt. Roger, like Ray Wilson and George Cohen, is sometimes seen as a supporting player in the World Cup story. I think this is partly because he was a naturally reticent man who kept his head down and just got on with it. He was one of the nicest people any of us ever knew, without a malicious bone in his body. He was incredibly relaxed. The only thing that unnerved him was an audience. After he retired he was less comfortable than some of us reminiscing about that day in front of a microphone or a camera. He did all his talking on the pitch.

Like Ray, Roger was first selected to play for England before Alf's time when he was still a Second Division player. He scored on his debut. 'A great header by Ralph Hunt!' said the commentator. He went to the 1962 World Cup. But while he won the League and the Cup with Liverpool, after four years he still didn't have that many caps to his name. He was left out six times by Alf and for five of them it was in favour of Jimmy Greaves. Only once did Alf pair them before 1966, against Portugal in the Little World Cup of 1964. As ever, Roger scored. He played for England four times that year and then only once in 1965, but that was the crucial win against Spain when the wingless experiment proved so effective. 'It was strange not seeing anyone on the wings,' Roger remarked. 'I wondered how it would work.' Without wings, and in a less attacking structure, he was released. His dynamism and nous came to the fore, and his capacity for hard work. More than Jimmy ever could or would, Roger put in a shift when possession had been lost. After that, he was rarely out of the team. And every time he was picked he carried on scoring, including in Madrid.

What Roger brought to the team along with his goals was lung power. The guy could run and run and run, and he just wouldn't stop. Take the iconic goal scored by Bobby Charlton against Mexico. Jack always liked to say that everyone talks about Bobby's spectacular shot, but what no one mentions is that the player who passed to him was Jack. It got him a big laugh every time, but it was absolute bollocks and Jack knew it. The ball was stabbed out of defence towards Roger, who saw Bobby advancing into the centre circle and slipped it across to him. And then he sprints off, driving a fast line deep into the inside-right position, causing a distraction as he drags a defender away and leaves only one stopper to stare like a rabbit in the headlights at Bobby as he surges unchallenged towards the penalty area. Before Bobby shoots, Roger cuts across the front of the box, sowing further confusion in the Mexican defence. He was like a minesweeper clearing space for Bobby to glide into. Bobby is remembered for the wondergoal, yes, but Roger helped create it. You wouldn't put his contribution on a highlights reel, but it made all the difference.

Then he scored the second against Mexico, had another one disallowed, and got two more against France. Jack could arguably take credit for making the first, but only because he missed a sitter by heading a lofted cross from Jimmy on the left onto the post. Roger was there to tap in the rebound. Then Cally crossed from the other wing and Roger's head was there to meet it. This was now his 15th goal in only his 16th cap. That's a strike rate to rival Messi or Ronaldo. It's certainly not a record that was going to get him dropped. At this point in the tournament, he was the joint top scorer along with Luis Artime of Argentina.

I'm amused by the reminder that Roger got one with his head against France. My sense is that at five foot nine he was no stronger in the air than Jimmy, who was five eight. In tandem, they didn't present defences with an aerial problem to solve. As Ray Wilson pithily said of Jimmy, 'he was bloody useless in the air'. I must have thought the same of Roger, because a year or two later I found myself ribbing him at an England get-together. 'Being smaller,' I said, 'have you ever scored a goal with your head?' He maybe didn't see that I was joking so he was slightly pissed off with this. When we met again at the next England game a few months later, he presented me with a list of all the goals he had scored with his head and included the result of the game. The header against France was there, and no doubt the header by 'Ralph Hunt' was too. By then, Roger was seven or eight years into his time with Liverpool, for whom he scored 285 goals, some presumably with his head. That phenomenal tally has only been beaten by Ian Rush, and he played a lot more games. Roger outscored Fowler, Dalglish, Owen and Keegan. Just before I started on this book Salah made it to 200, with Roger's benchmark still a long way off.

Anyway, my question clearly touched a nerve. 'While you were up front scoring all the goals and grabbing all the headlines,' he added, 'I was tracking back doing all your fucking defensive work.'

I can't argue with that. But he was smiling when he said it. We gelled straight away, and I loved being paired up front with him.

Could England have won the World Cup without Roger? We'll never know but the reality is that Alf was never inclined to find out. In later life, Jimmy theorised that if anyone was going to be dropped to accommodate him, it would have been Roger to go rather than me. Well, maybe. They were both such great players that it has taken me a very long time to understand that, in picking me for the final, Alf made the right decision. Three into two wouldn't go.

For his part, Roger always felt that he could never win a popularity contest with Jimmy. Before the World Cup the press didn't want him to claim Jimmy's place, and after it the public never quite forgave him for having done so.

But there was always respect between them. And that showed at one of the reunion tour events we did in front of a big audience. Roger, like Ray, was happy to turn up and come on stage to take the applause so long as he wasn't expected to say anything. He was fearless on the pitch, putting his body on the line without a care for danger, and yet he had a paralysing terror of public speaking. In that sense, he was the opposite of Jimmy, who alongside Terry Baker was co-hosting this particular show with all his usual charm and swagger.

The structure of the show was that everyone onstage had to speak for five minutes, though Roger as usual was exempted. Then suddenly he decided he wanted to say something. So he took hold of the microphone. As he did so I could see his hand shaking with nerves.

'No one's mentioned our compère tonight,' he said.

And Roger Hunt launched into a powerful and heartfelt tribute to Jimmy Greaves, England's greatest ever goalscorer.

16
THE D WORD

R ecently I was watching a documentary about a teammate. There have been a few of them over the years.
I've seen most and I've been in a few of them too. But this one
was different. Although I wasn't in it, I was mentioned.

Finding Jack Charlton, first broadcast in 2020 just a few
months after Jack passed away, was a portrait of a great man
diminished by old age. But some details had survived: while he
could no longer remember names, he still knew faces.

'You don't know how much they take in,' his wife Pat
explained. 'If you said to him, "Geoff Hurst," he'll look and go,
"Who?" But if he met Geoff he'd know him.'

I hadn't seen Jack for a while but I had heard about his
illness. The sad truth is that the news came as no surprise. In
its various forms, dementia had been stalking my old teammates for many years. Typically, Jack found the perfect words to
encapsulate the illness's cruelty.

'I couldn't remember a lot of the memories,' he said.

'Never mind,' said Pat.

I suspect that I ignored the early signs when I first came
across them during one of the golf days. I was playing a three-
ball with Jack and Nobby. After we finished playing a hole, there
was a short walk from the green to the next tee. Two things

happened. When we got to the tee Jack realised that he'd inadvertently left his clubs behind so he went back to get them. By the time he had reached the tee again, Nobby had teed off a second time. Maybe it's a defence mechanism that stops you worrying about the potential seriousness of the situation, but the early evidence of dementia can produce these moments that you dismiss because they're amusing. Now that I think about it, these were clear early indications in not one but in two of my teammates. But at the time they wouldn't necessarily have been clear to me. We're all forgetful. Crikey, look at me!

We've had an epidemic of it in my generation of players. The first to be claimed by dementia was Jeff Astle. Not that this was publicly stated at the time. I got to know Jeff when he was selected by Alf Ramsey for the squad that went to Mexico for the World Cup in 1970. He was a funny man, and a great guy to be around, as viewers discovered from his popular appearances with Frank Skinner and David Baddiel on *Fantasy Football League* in the 1990s. One of his five caps was against Brazil in that epic group game remembered for Gordon Banks's save from Pelé and Bobby Moore's tackle on Jairzinho – not to mention Jairzinho's sensational winner so coolly set up by Pelé. It's not a fair reflection of the great career Jeff had at West Brom that he is partly remembered for snapping a side-footed shot past the far post in that game. As a player he was immensely strong in the air. There's a brilliant photograph of Jeff, which captures him in mid-flight as he throws himself into a diving header. His head is almost disappearing into the leather. They don't make footballers like that any more. Or, thank goodness, footballs.

Though medical science has never conclusively proved as much, it is widely assumed that for footballers of my vintage, heading was the root of much evil. When Jeff died at the age of 59 in 2002, he had been suffering from dementia for up to five years. At the inquest, the coroner found the cause of death to be repeated head traumas. The verdict was death by industrial injury. In other words, football killed him.

The causal link between heading and dementia still hasn't been scientifically established. But it has been claimed that a footballer is three and a half times more likely to suffer from dementia than a regular person in the street. Nor is there any research about the particular impact of heading a heavily waterlogged leather ball. That was a reality of football in the wet winters of my career. Collectively, the evidence of my team-mates makes a strong case for the prosecution. Jack and Jeff, in particular, headed the ball almost as often as they kicked it. I suppose it begs the question: what about me?

I headed a lot of balls. In a match, I may only have done so two or three times, but with the innovation of the near-post cross there was a lot of practice on the training ground. To get good at it, we had to put in our so-called 10,000 hours. Then there was the gym. We had a ball hanging from the ceiling and I would practise on it all the time. As for younger players, I'm glad that in 2020 guidelines were introduced limiting the amount of heading done in training by under 18s. To me that makes sense. By all means practise crossing, but a young player doesn't need to get on the end of every cross on the training ground.

I am not convinced that I joined the dots following Jeff's inquest. But not long after he died, I was with many of my old teammates at a signing event at a big conference-type venue in Birmingham. It was a weekend job, taking up the whole of the Saturday and the Sunday. Most of us were there, and it proved a great success. Halfway through the weekend, on the Saturday night, we were all eating together. I was sitting opposite Ray Wilson when out of the blue he courageously dropped into the conversation that he had a diagnosis of Alzheimer's. I remember being surprised, both that he was so open about it, and also that he had any such illness at all. I didn't see Ray on a regular basis, and had not realised that he was showing any early signs. It was a mark of his esteem for the group that he felt he could tell us. He wasn't with a bunch of strangers.

Ray found out in 2004. In retirement he kept up with his walking. He hiked the big trails in the north of England – the Pennine Way and the Coast to Coast Walk. But after a while, as the illness took a grip, he preferred to keep to the familiar environment of home. The last public appearance that I can think of is in 2008 at the BBC Sports Personality of the Year, when Bobby Charlton won his lifetime achievement award. As his best friend in the England set-up, Ray wanted to be there and cried his eyes out as Bobby paid tribute to his teammates. But after a certain point we no longer saw him at the golf days. According to his wife Pat, he never lost his inner joy, filling his days with constant sketching and doodling, and laughing and singing almost to the end, which came in 2018.

In 2011 Peter Bonetti was diagnosed with dementia. I remember him as an incredibly daring goalkeeper who was fearless in diving at the feet of strikers. This would have repeatedly put his head in danger. After his death, his brother revealed that Peter had also headed the ball a lot in training when taking part in games as an outfield player. So, a double whammy. He was there for the golf day at Brocton Hall in 2013, smiling in the group photo. He didn't make what turned out to be the last gathering in 2016, and passed away four years later. That summer of 2016 someone visiting a West Midlands hospital for older patients with mental health difficulties happened to recognise Peter in one of the beds. They found him watching a video of the Chelsea–Leeds FA Cup final from 1970.

Then there was Nobby. Despite seeing him tee off twice from the same hole, I probably didn't take the threat as seriously as I might have if I'd seen him more often. It only became clearer to me that he was also suffering from a form of dementia when one year we were booked to do an after-dinner speaking event together. Within our tight circle, the rest of us had heard that he was struggling, but he still did social evenings with his son John operating as a chaperone. On the evening we were due to appear together, the three of us were waiting in a private room before we went on stage. John's presence was obviously necessary to Nobby – he helped him a fair bit with answering questions. But at one point John announced that he was leaving the room to make sure that everything had been organised, ready for our appearance. Perhaps John assumed that Nobby would feel comfortable in the company of someone he'd known for 40 years. But as soon as he left the room, Nobby started to show signs of deep discomfort and real agitation. He got up out of his seat and tried to walk out of the door. I tried my best to soothe him, reassuring him that John would be back in a minute. He really only calmed down once John returned.

As soon as we went onstage, nobody in the audience would have known beyond the fact that Nobby needed a bit of prompting from John. But to see the transformation in an old friend who was always so chirpy disturbed and saddened me. Exposed to it at close quarters for the first time, I started to understand how serious the condition can be.

No teammate was closer to me than Martin Peters. Again, the evidence presented itself on one of the golf days. I was playing in a three-ball with Martin and Roger Hunt. At a certain point in our round, Martin suddenly announced that he wanted to get off the course. He obviously wasn't feeling well, though it wasn't clear to me what his symptoms were. Certainly he seemed confused. So I decided to accompany him back to the clubhouse. It was quite alarming to sit next to him as he attempted to steer the buggy. He almost drove into two or three bunkers, it was that bad. But eventually I got him back to the dressing room, helped him get changed, and stayed with him until he could be reunited with Kathy.

There was a lighter side to that afternoon. Roger was left on his own on the course and, not knowing that I wouldn't be able to rejoin the game, he waited for me. To pass the time he started practising his chips. Another four-ball came up from the previous hole and, as he politely waved them through, one of them approached and said, 'You know you can't play this golf course on your own.' Roger explained the situation and they moved through the hole. Then another four-ball came up and someone else said exactly the same thing. Roger got really fucking annoyed, which I found highly amusing when he told me over drinks before dinner. They wouldn't have said it to a

Charlton, but Roger was such an unassuming guy they almost certainly had no idea they were talking to a World Cup winner.

In 2013, Martin duly became the third player in our team to be diagnosed with Alzheimer's. For me, this was different. My wife Judith had known his wife Kathy since they were both 17. They began talking every day when they became neighbours in the mid-1960s, and they still talk every day now. Kathy suspected Martin had been suffering from dementia for a good three years already, but over the course of six further gruelling years we had sad daily bulletins from Kathy as ever so gradually the great friend I'd known so well disappeared into the disease.

The announcement that Martin had Alzheimer's wasn't actually made until 2016. The year is significant, as it brought the last hurrah of the team on the 50th anniversary of the 1966 World Cup. That's when we started to say goodbye to one another, and the public got a final glimpse of some – though sadly not all – of us together. It started in January where, half a century on from the draw for the World Cup, Martin, Gordon Banks, George Cohen and I attended a celebration and were snapped with a copy of the Jules Rimet trophy. That summer at Wimbledon, Bobby Charlton and I sat next to each other in the Royal Box one sunny afternoon as guests of the All England Lawn Tennis and Croquet Club. Banksy was also there. In turn, we all enjoyed the warm appreciation of the crowd as we stood up to be introduced to the Centre Court.

My last public appearance with Bobby came a few weeks later at Wembley Arena. In front of an audience of 10,000, we reminisced about the big day in the stadium next door. Then in the evening there was a dinner attended by several members of the squad, who also came back for the Community Shield game between Man U and those folk heroes of Leicester City. The last event of the year was a quieter one, in October. I was one of the squad invited to open Sir Alf Ramsey Way at the FA's national football centre at St George's Park in Burton-on-Trent. The other teammates who could make it were Jimmy Armfield, Norman Hunter, Roger Hunt and George Cohen.

There's no getting away from the fact that, half a century on from our sporting prime, we were old men. None was as medically challenged as George. He was physically the strongest player in the team but in the mid-1970s he was diagnosed with bowel cancer, which returned in 1980. One oncologist even advised him to get his affairs in order. His wife Daphne said, 'George is going nowhere,' and she nursed him and nursed him and nursed him. It was many years before he was declared free of it. Through her support and his strength of character, he had survived. By now, he was pushing 80 and walking with the aid of a stick, but to me he seemed indestructible. I spoke to him before the event and he told me that he and Daphne were going to get there early. So I said, 'OK, we'll get there the night before and meet and have a meal.' We hadn't seen him before the four of us sat down, when he explained that he'd asked for a room fairly close to reception so he wouldn't have to walk too far. Despite this request, the room turned out to be quite a hike away. So that was one inconvenience. Undaunted, George struggled all the way there. Opened the door. Lovely room. 'Only one problem,' he said. 'We couldn't see a bed. It's obviously a modern hotel. Push a button somewhere and a bed will come down.' George had suffered greater indignities and had a wry sense of humour. But it turned out there really was no bed. He was entitled to say, 'Don't you know who I am?' but was far too down to earth to kick up a fuss. I won't embarrass the hotel by naming it.

The first of us to go was our captain in 1993. Having already kept a secret of his testicular cancer in the 1960s, Bobby Moore was just as quiet about his bowel cancer. But I knew he was ill and towards the end went to visit him in hospital after he'd had a really serious operation. Either his condition was still bad, or he was in no state to receive visitors, or his family were trying to preserve his dignity, but they wouldn't let me see him. I admit I was bitterly disappointed. Perhaps this was a final act of exclusion from a man who, for all his life, had emotionally kept himself shielded from others. I knew he didn't have long – this was within a week or two of his death – and it's a great sadness to me that I wasn't able to say goodbye. The news came across on the radio as I was driving up the M1. Even though I was prepared for the worst, when the shock came it still hit me hard. However much your head may accept that a death is imminent, it's as if your heart has no idea. I remember that I'd just passed a service station so there was no pulling in. I just had to carry on driving, knowing that the greatest footballer I've ever played with, the giant I held on my shoulder that afternoon long ago, was no more. At the next service station I stopped and had a coffee, and have never felt more relieved not to be recognised. He was 51.

Fittingly for a national treasure, Mooro's memorial service was held at Westminster Abbey. Judith and Claire accompanied me to hear Bobby speak from the pulpit and Franz Beckenbauer read from Ecclesiastes. There was a pew left empty for Alf Ramsey, who by now was suffering from dementia. Martin, who lived in Essex, would regularly visit Alf at his home in Ipswich and so witnessed his slow disappearance until the memories of 1966 had faded altogether. Alf's memorial in 1999 was scandalously under-attended by the officials of the game. But seven of the team were there and George paid a wonderful tribute to him. 'I know I speak for the entire 1966 World Cup squad when I say that Alf's influence changed our lives,' he said. 'Not just for what we achieved under him but for the enrichment of our lives for having known and played for him.'

In 2004, the year of Ray's diagnosis, Alan Ball lost his childhood sweetheart Lesley to ovarian cancer. That time I played golf with him in Australia, he decided to go on a long trip Down Under so as not to have to be in the house on his own. He stayed with the same friend who hosted Judith and me. I have a vivid image of him spending a little bit of every day carefully sweeping around the swimming pool. He was 61 when in 2007 he too died, from a heart attack. Many of us made our mournful way to his funeral in Winchester Cathedral, where his flat cap and the flag of St George adorned the coffin.

And then we were nine. Of those nine, six would go on to be claimed by one form of dementia or another. It was a solemn day when Roger's wife Rowan phoned to inform us that he too had been diagnosed. Judith spoke to him on the phone a couple of times but, the golf reunions being over, we were never to see him again. Banksy and George died of other causes. Later came Jack and then, the final blow, Bobby. Long before his illness was announced I had started to suspect that he was not well because in games at Old Trafford the television cameras stopped cutting to the familiar shot of the great man in his seat.

Before and then, increasingly, after the golden anniversary in 2016, the surviving members of the 1966 squad started to fall. John Connelly died in 2012, Ron Springett and Gerry Byrne in 2015, Ray Wilson and Jimmy Armfield in 2018, Gordon Banks and Martin Peters in 2019, Jack Charlton, Nobby Stiles, Peter Bonetti and Norman Hunter in 2020, Roger Hunt, Jimmy Greaves and Ron Flowers in 2021, George Cohen in 2022, Bobby Charlton in 2023. Three months after Bobby died, I was contacted by Susanne Tilkowski. She had informed me of the death of her father Hans, aged 84, just before the pandemic in 2020. Now she texted the news that Franz Beckenbauer had gone too. The latest member of German team to pass away is Karl-Heinz Schnellinger, who passed away at 85 while this book was in the late stages of preparation.

I went to all the funerals I could. I felt a wrench every time I couldn't. Some I missed because of the pandemic. I spoke at Banksy's. I had my own medical issue preventing me from making it to Roger's, but had a message kindly read out by Ian Callaghan. The last one I actually attended was Martin's in Brentwood. His ashes are interred beneath the statue of him and me holding up Mooro that I helped unveil at the London Stadium in 2021. I suppose that this was my very final goodbye to a teammate.

I now find it deeply distressing whenever I look at the pictures of us all together, particularly the ones taken at Lilleshall and at Roehampton when we had the tournament still ahead of us. In blue tracksuits, or in red shirts and white shorts, in suits, in one press call even wearing our club kits, together we looked into the lens, fit young men in our footballing prime, none of us knowing what might unfold in the coming days and weeks, let alone years and decades.

At the time of writing, I may be the last of the XI who played in the final, but Cally, Terry Paine and George Eastham are still here. Long may they remain so. I don't think about this often, but sometimes I wonder if I'll survive long enough to become the very oldest member of the winning team. Of those to go in their eighties, Banksy was 81, Roger, Ray and George were 83. The Charlton brothers survived the longest: Jack died at the age of 85 and Bobby had just turned 86. I was the last player to be picked for the World Cup XI when Alf called me up to face Argentina. If I make it to Christmas 2027, I will be the senior pro.

Whether I do or not, let's see. My back gets a bit stiff when I've been sitting for too long. I don't suppose I could give any man-markers the slip these days, but I try to walk for an hour every day. While working on this book there's been the odd scare. One was minor, one wasn't.

The first happened when I was touring my theatre show. People who come to it are nice and complimentary and tell me I am looking well. Then at a performance in Frome I had a nosebleed and, because I couldn't staunch the flow, the show had to be cancelled after 15 minutes. News of it got out into the press and I was inundated with calls and messages asking me if I was OK. It turned out to be no more than an inconvenience, and several weeks later I was able to go back to Frome and get through the show without mishap.

Then, when I was reaching the end of this process of gathering together my memories, I started to feel a very serious discomfort all over my chest. It was a Monday morning and we were due to collect our granddaughter Grace and take her to stage school. Straight afterwards, I was due to have a meeting in Cheltenham about this book. I went into the bedroom and told Judith I wasn't feeling great. I wouldn't say I felt terrible, it wasn't the worst pain I've ever felt, but I was sweating profusely and lay down on the bed. Judith was brilliant. Without panicking she called 111, got nowhere and instead dialled 999. They told her to give me an aspirin to chew and, if I stopped breathing, to turn me on my side.

An ambulance with two paramedics arrived within ten minutes. When they took my shirt off it was wringing wet. They kept telling me to relax, which proved a lot easier once they'd given me morphine.

Judith fielded their questions. How old was I? 82. One paramedic was kind enough to express surprise. 'Can you believe how old he is?' he said when three more paramedics arrived in a second ambulance. The extra crew were needed in case they couldn't fit a wheelchair into the lift and they'd have to carry me down four flights of stairs. This proved unnecessary. As well as my age, the other topic of interest was our flat. 'This is posh,' said one of them. In the ambulance another paramedic admitted to Judith that he had a snoop around.

None of them seemed to recognise me. Judith likes to tease me that I was bitterly disappointed, that I was lying there with a pen at the ready. 'Haven't you told them, Jude?' Mercifully the closest I got to answering questions about the World Cup was when a doctor at Cheltenham General asked if I wished to be addressed as Sir Geoffrey.

'Geoff's fine,' I said, as usual.

But I very nearly wasn't fine. It turns out I had suffered a heart attack.

They put a catheter in my arm and on a screen were soon showing me three of the arteries feeding into my heart. Two were OK and one was blocked. By this time, Joanne and Charlotte had joined their mother at the hospital and so they were all informed together that I'd had two stents inserted and an artery unblocked, and that I was staying in for at least a couple of nights.

Not for one second did I think: this is it. As I lay in a cardiac ward for two days, the boredom was relieved by visits from three of my grandchildren. Grace was very nervous that I was going to look like a wreck. 'He's a lot better today than yesterday,' her mother told her. 'He has wires all over him.'

Eventually they let me go home with a booklet full of dos and don'ts, and within a fortnight I went up north to do a couple of speaking engagements. It's Judith's opinion that I want to die onstage. She adds that there have been a few times when I already have!

As the last boy of '66, I sometimes wonder if I'm seen as the lone survivor of a species facing extinction. But when the time does come for my own funeral, my preference is for no fuss. I don't want the press outside taking snaps of dignitaries with long faces. I don't want representatives of the FA or FIFA or even West Ham. In fact, I just want my family to be there: my two daughters, my five grandchildren, my son-in-law.

And my wife. This is if I predecease her, of course! Selfishly, I hope I do, because after our 60 years together I can't imagine life without her.

The reason is simple. Judith has been such a loyal companion. Through all these years she has had to live with someone comfortable being in the public eye. But the limelight is not for her. She tolerated her moment in the sun the day after the final when we had a picture taken in Kensington Gardens, and there are those lovely snaps of her carrying my man-of-the-match cup. Since 1966 – apart from that brief cameo in Mexico four years later – she has stayed away from the public gaze. A very private person, she has generously made room for the fame that came with that hattrick all those years ago. To insist that she and our family are left to mourn in peace will be my final act of thanks.

The crazy thing about our profession is that, whenever I do go, the news is likely to make the bulletins and even the odd front page. The goals from the last big game to be broadcast in black and white will be shown again. The header from Mooro's clever free kick. The right-foot shot on the turn from indefatigable Bally's cross. The left-foot lash after Mooro's ice-cool chip upfield. But before the final whistle blows, there's more to say about the game than those three moments. Much more.

17

AND HERE COMES HURST

I awoke on 30 July 1966 with no thought that the coming hours would mark me for life. We could win, or we could lose. If the two teams could not be separated after extra time there would be a replay. After that the toss of a coin. I didn't think it would come to that. With a team that had Bobby Moore and Bobby Charlton, Ray Wilson and Gordon Banks, I thought we would probably win. Even with no Jimmy Greaves. The only person to have a hunch about my own contribution was Jack Harries.

My father-in-law had seen me score plenty of goals at Upton Park that season. He now predicted to Judith that by the end of the afternoon I would have a hattrick to my name. I didn't hear about it till after, but I can't say I would have greeted it as a prophecy from Nostradamus. One man to get three against West Germany? They'd let in only two goals so far, and they'd scored 13. We'd got seven. He could have got bloody good odds.

I got up and got ready. Some of the boys walked to the shops in Hendon and encountered the odd well-wisher. I don't recall how I whiled away the morning beyond reading the papers and pondering what boots to wear. Longer screw-in studs, I reckoned, to counteract the effect of overnight rain. A photograph from the day captures me at a midday lunch in the hotel dining room with some of the squad. Alone among my teammates, for some reason I turn my face towards the camera. Perhaps my selection ahead of Jimmy made me the story on the morning of the final. I don't know. I look serious, but I wouldn't read too much into my expression. Martin Peters gnaws his lip and looks incredibly young. Bobby Charlton seems much more pensive. Perhaps he'd just been given his instructions. For the good of the team, Alf told him he must spend the afternoon keeping an eye on Franz Beckenbauer. The biggest game of his life and England's greatest ever attacking player, scorer of the howitzer against Mexico and two brilliant goals in the semi-final, was instructed to do a man-marking job. He had never once man-marked in his entire career.

Soon we boarded the team bus, to be sent on our way by a crowd of thousands. The closer we drew to the stadium, the now familiar route from the hotel was ever more thickly lined with cheering crowds. We'd had this for the semi too, but today there were more. This is the bonus and the burden of hosting a tournament: you can see the hopes of the nation written on countless faces in the streets.

With an hour and a quarter till kick-off, the vehicle descended into the bowels of Wembley. The stadium was still far from full as some players sauntered out onto the pitch to check the state of the turf and make a final decision about studs. After I met Judith, her dad and my parents and gave them their tickets, we made our way to the dressing room only to discover a throng of administrators and media, a film crew, photographers and assorted hangers-on. This felt weird and very un-Alf-like, but I seem to remember taking the hullaballoo in my stride, staying in my mental space, until they were cleared out and then the rest of the squad left to take their seats and the 11 of us were alone. Hanging on pegs around the room were ten red shirts and one yellow one. Alf and his team did all they could to help us get into the zone. In the silences you could hear the rumble of nearly 100,000 voices above. Closer by was the sound of Bally not talking for the first time in forever.

Alf had said we were going to win the World Cup, and over the course of three and a half years he had done all he could to find 11 Englishmen in a specific mould. He liked his footballers to be hard workers, team players, cool heads. But he couldn't rule out psychological quirks altogether. Beyond the usual fiddling with kit and tweaking of laces that obsesses all players before games, most had their own habits and routines. Every morning of the World Cup, Nobby rose early, trying not to wake his roommate, and walked down to Golders Green where he had found a Catholic church among the many synagogues. While this daily duty was an expression of his religious faith, Nobby talked about it as a type of superstition too. He worried that not to go to mass each morning could reverse the team's run of luck. And he was up with the lark to say his prayers this morning.

Others had their own rituals. In those days there was no limbering up on the pitch, so in his socks George would do about 50 or 60 knees up in the dressing room in front of everybody. Banksy liked bouncing a ball against the wall to get the feel of it. He also had a specific brand of beechnut gum he would chew before smearing sugary saliva all over his hands to make them more adhesive. It almost went horribly wrong before the semi-final when Harold Shepherdson, who acted as his supplier, confessed at the last minute that he didn't have any. Alf ordered him off to the shops to buy some and a wheezing Shep arrived back in the tunnel with the right gum in the nick of time. Today, because of the threat of rain, Banksy was wearing gloves. Jack applied Vaseline to his eyebrows. Ray smeared Vicks VapoRub round his nostrils. In a routine they kept to for the whole World Cup, he also handed the same broken-topped inhaler to Bobby who always took one huff of ammonia. Mooro, once Shep had rubbed liniment into his legs, was as ever the last person in the team to pull on his shorts.

I had no quirks whatsoever. No superstitions, no rituals, no good-luck tricks that I had developed to help turn the game our way. My final act after pulling on my red shirt was a prac-tical one. I carefully plucked out my false front tooth. I'd been doing this ever since, one day aged 20 or so, I went out to bat for Chelmsford and a rising ball knocked out an incisor as if it were a middle stump, sending it 15 yards off to square leg. Nobby had already removed his upper dentures and given them to Ian Callaghan to look after. He also took off his thick-rimmed glasses and put in his contacts, squirting them with fluid. This was always quite a performance, and you couldn't get anywhere near him when he was in the middle of it. Also, he nipped off to the loo more than once, bless him.

It was time. We all shook hands, Nobby and Bally almost certainly made some noise and, studs clattering, we emerged into the long corridor that led towards the mouth of the tunnel. We formed a line. In the claret and blue of West Ham, Martin liked to be the last man in the team to walk onto the pitch, but this was Jack's preference too and as he was older he claimed priority. One of four in the team carrying a ball, I stood behind Ray and in front of Bobby, the two most capped players in the team.

And here, coming out of the dressing room opposite and lining up to our left, were the Germans. They'd won the toss and chosen to wear their home kit. White shirts with thick black trim. Black shorts. White socks. Among them, blue eyes and blond heads.

There's no point in not saying that, in 1966, the Second World War was barely yet a memory. It had come to an end just 21 years earlier. That's only as far back as the 2003 war in Iraq is at the time of writing. This was not a rematch – of course it wasn't – and I'm not saying that any of us was driven by a personal animosity towards our opponents, because we weren't. But the recent past was there, whether we liked it or not. For us, for them, for the crowd. All but one of our team had been born in the era of the Third Reich. Alan Ball, the exception, arrived four days after VE Day. Aside from Franz Beckenbauer, a skinny boy of 20 now looking into the eyes of Bobby Charlton, the same applied to the Germans. The war was part of our life story. Nobby was born during a bombing raid on Manchester. Banksy remembered the cold of wartime winters because the Luftwaffe had warped the window frames. Martin was evacuated from east London to Shropshire. One night in the Blitz the family of his wife Kathy was decimated by a single bomb. Judith's father was a paratrooper who took part in the heroic battle to disable the Merville gun battery near Sword Beach on D-Day. He wasn't a fan of Germans. Maybe it was this that made him foretell a hattrick for his son-in-law.

The mouth of the tunnel gaped above us. Beyond you could hear thunder, but not see the source of it. I had nothing to compare this to. Not my two finals here for West Ham. Not even the quarter-final and the semi-final. They were stepping stones and now 22 of us had reached football's ultimate destination. For years, I've compared the intensity of the moment to being caught in the backdraft of a fire. But there are fires and there are fires, and this felt like being on the edge of an inferno that sucked you towards it. Up there, at the end of the slope rising into the light, all England seemed to wait, to expect.

Then up at the front there was movement. The referee Gottfried Dienst of Switzerland, the linesmen Karol Galba of Czechoslovakia and Tofiq Bahramov of the Soviet Union, began to walk. Slowly 11 Germans and 11 Englishmen together filed up into the glare and the roar.

Seeler, Tilkowski, Schnellinger, Beckenbauer, Schulz, Emmerich, Weber, Haller, Held, Overath, Höttges.

Moore, Cohen, Ball, Banks, Hunt, Wilson, Hurst, R. Charlton, Peters, Stiles, J. Charlton.

There were the formalities. The anthems, the introductions, the handshakes. Her Majesty and FIFA VIPs. Mooro did his little signal to Tina. As Judith knew, I wasn't thinking of her, nor our little girl Claire being looked after by her grandmother, nor my parents in the crowd, nor my brother Robert in a young offenders institution. My mind certainly wasn't on the hundreds of millions watching elsewhere on the planet. My head was filled only with thoughts of the 90 minutes to come.

I'd played against West Germany in my full debut only five months earlier. Ours was pretty much the same team then and now. Just five of the Germans had survived. One of them was the keeper. Tilkowski. I knew we were the same height and I knew I was going to let him know I was there. As for who'd be marking me, I liked to give a bit of thought to who I'd be up against and tailor the way I played accordingly. If it was an older guy I might run him around a lot to try and knacker him out. If it was someone who wasn't so strong in the air I'd be sure to spend a lot of time on the far post. Schulz I knew would play as a sweeper. Having done my homework, I was expecting them to put Weber on me because as a chunky stopper he was my natural match-up. But straight after the kick-off Weber went across and stood near Roger. Schnellinger attached himself to Bally. Beckenbauer, it turned out, had been instructed to stay on Bobby. The player who latched on to me was the right back Höttges. So I was going to be tailed by a marker who was two inches shorter and not primarily a stopper.

In that moment, I very clearly remember thinking that I was going to have a pretty good game.

To revisit the story of this mythic final after so long, I decide to sit down and watch it. I haven't done this half as much as people might suspect. While I've always told myself that I know the game well, I want to wipe away the film of dust and see it afresh. I am amazed to find it contains surprises.

To start with, there's the openness, the sheer stretch of the play. The two defensive lines lie far less close to each other than they would today, which means the midfield contains more space than we are used to seeing now. It gives the players of yesteryear time to think and to speculate. Nobby, so long remembered as a terrier who darted about tackling people, has room to go forward and show what he can do. He gets even more time on the ball because Bobby has Beckenbauer sticking to him like a dance partner. I love the way Jack nips upfield, more fleet of foot than he's ever thought to be, laying off passes and interlinking like a proper footballer. George chunters up and down the wing all afternoon, those powerful thighs of his pumping with energy. Only one of his crosses lands, as his Fulham teammate Bobby Robson once joked, among the photographers.

We're not flawless though.

The first goal, when it comes in the 12th minute, is silly and soft and mortifying for Ray but I don't think I would have been overly concerned. That's true of all the players, including Jack and Banksy who watch Haller's scuffed shot bobble inside the far post.

England 0 West Germany 1.

There is a long way to go and it's far from the end of the world. Instead of one, we're just going to have to get two.

I sense that I have the beating of Tilkowski early on when we both go up for a cross. I leap much higher than him and get punched in the face. Nowadays a successor to Herr Dienst would no doubt whistle and probably even show me a yellow card. But in 1966 it is a legitimate challenge. While Tilkowski gives me a black eye, I put a dent in his confidence. He's on the floor for a minute and half receiving treatment. When he rises, he looks dazed and is spattered in mud. I'm thinking: *I've softened him up.* He can't be that hurt because he is soon turning a fine shot on the left from Martin round the far post. Not long before half time he makes an even better save from Roger, shooting closer in on the same angle. But for the rest of the game he's wobbly in the air.

On 18 minutes Mooro is fouled by Overath inside their half on the left. He doesn't hang about. Sniffing opportunity, he places the ball quickly, looks up, feints, then strokes a weighted chip 30 yards upfield towards the near post. He'd put the ball on the same sixpence a thousand times in training at Chadwell Heath, the idea being to create danger in an area of the box where traditionally none existed. The back post was where defenders were used to defending aerially and that's where I loiter now until suddenly, just as Mooro knows I will, I dart across the edge of the six-yard box and come to meet the incoming ball. The Germans should know this is a signature of mine – they've seen the Argentina game – but I'm not followed. Höttges is nowhere. Tilkowski is rooted on the line. Without anyone to challenge me, I rise, hang in the air for a split second as I wait for the ball to meet my forehead, and then with a jerk of my neck I stab it down to the right of Tilkowski, who doesn't move a muscle.

England 1 West Germany 1.

I remember with absolute clarity the thought that entered my head as I run off the pitch, turn and, standing in front of the photographers, leap into the air. In my first ever game for England, one pundit had said I looked lost up front. Where was Hurst? The nagging thought that I don't belong has never quite left me. So far, I have been playing as if still auditioning. However important it proved, the goal in the quarter-final was no more than progress. The same went for setting up the winner in the semi. In a flash, and with a goal that has West Ham United written all over it, I have this incredibly powerful feeling. Until I met Mooro's free kick I had not justified my place in the team. I have now. The ridiculous celebration says as much. These days, when they're not knee-sliding or slapping the badge on their chests, players seem to work out their goal celebrations with the help of a choreographer. Not me. I am so overjoyed I jump up like an ecstatic five-year-old, drawing both knees up in front of me and shaking my arms. It's the stupidest and most embarrassing goal celebration of my entire career. But it captures a feeling. I have arrived. I am soon hugged by Martin and Roger and Bobby, and then I jog back for the restart, trying to process a new thought.

I belong in the England team. Finally.

It has been a scrappy game. West Germany have looked more dangerous and we haven't performed particularly well. But there won't be another goal for a whole hour now. So, as I watch nearly 60 years later, I settle back and look for themes. Another thing I see anew is the flexibility. People associate the 1960s with positional rigidity, but within our allotted roles Alf encouraged free thinking. Bobby gets everywhere trying to lose his marker, driving left and right, drilling and lofting even more passes with his left foot than his right. Bally and Martin must be an absolute nightmare to play against, swapping flanks at the drop of a hat, coming inside, popping up here, there and everywhere. Roger and I never stop running after hopeful balls sent forward for us to chase and turn defenders.

Meanwhile at the back, Mooro is Mooro, reading the game with that sixth sense of his, snuffing out problems with half an eye always on getting something going. He's so calm that sometimes you barely notice him. Then five minutes from half time Emmerich is through. It's their best chance since the goal until Mooro strides across and slides in with a covering tackle. The stadium salutes him.

As I watch, it's interesting to see quite how often both teams shoot from distance. Was this an instruction from the managers? Or nerves? Maybe without Jimmy on the pitch there was less of an impetus to get the ball to him to work his magic inside the box. Martin is letting off long-range potshots as if he's on a performance-related bonus, but he hasn't got his shooting boots on today. He didn't score many from distance for West Ham either, to be frank, so I'm not sure what's going on in his head. Roger and I have no luck either and even Bobby isn't often on target. George, who is very right-footed, sends a left-foot effort spiralling away towards the corner flag.

I don't know why the Germans bother shooting from distance, which they do more and more as the game goes on. You didn't beat Banksy from range. You didn't often get past him nearer either. This is well illustrated in a passage of play ten minutes before half time when George, guilty of overthinking, gets into a right old mess with Held and Jack marches over to snuff out the problem. From the cleared corner, Overath whacks a shot from outside the box. Banksy parries it into the path of Emmerich and then safely gathers his close-range drive into his midriff. No drama, no problem, no goal. Minutes later he makes a flying save from Seeler.

Despite all the talk of Beckenbauer, for me the great player of the German side is the captain. This is Seeler's third World Cup. He doesn't necessarily look like a natural athlete but he's a hell of a footballer, strong and skilful and always asking questions. Beckenbauer shows every sign that he will grow into one of the greats. At 20 his composure in defence and going forward is already there. Overath, who will also go on to play in three World Cups, is a persistent creative threat too.

It's lovely to be reminded that the game is played in a very good spirit. Jack gets into a rage when he's whistled for handball after chesting down a through pass. Mooro has the odd growl too. Nobby does a Nobby special on Haller, sliding in late after the ball is dinked past him. Bally gets right in there to pacify the ref and keep his roommate out of trouble. But I don't see any players arguing with the opposition. There's a lot of courtesy. Civil pats on the shoulder. Gentlemanly handshakes. Everyone is on their best behaviour.

As the match goes on it's exhausting just to watch. This isn't the world of careful possession football where teams keep hold of the ball for minutes on end and get nowhere. The game ebbs and flows from end to end from start to finish. To me it's what football should look like.

It opens up even more after half time. When we get back to the dressing room, Alf tells Roger to stop tracking back so much and give Schulz something to think about. So there's ever more space in midfield to play with. We come back out to a pitch drenched by a sudden shower, and the going gets tough. The turf cuts up and both boxes begin to look as if a steeplechase has just galloped through. I don't mind at all because it's harder for a defender to judge things on an uneven pitch. Plus I've played on much, much worse in the English midwinter.

We sense we've got the beating of them. We look fluid and we look fit. That fortnight at Lilleshall is paying off. And Bally is starting to motor.

With 20 minutes to go, Tilkowski is on the deck again. It's not my fault, guv, not this time. I meet a cross, nodding it towards the far post, and when Tilkowski goes up for it he collides with Beckenbauer. He gets back up grimacing and clutching an ear.

We probe and we probe and then, with the clock ticking towards 80, Bobby half-beats Beckenbauer with a burst of speed. The ball comes to Roger, sleeves rolled up and shoulders hunched, who feeds a beautiful pass inside Schnellinger for Bally to run on to and whip a low shot which Tilkowski turns round the post.

The crowd senses something. They're chanting 'England, England' now.

Bally's corner grazes the head of Schulz and falls to me outside the box. I jig away from Seeler, shoot, catch the leg of Höttges and up loops the ball. And there he is. The Ghost.

England 2 West Germany 1.

Roger is first to hug Martin. When I wrap him in my arms too, the camera looking over his shoulder captures my gap-toothed grin that says everything. Relief. Joy. Confidence that we've got this thing in the bag now. We're going to win the World Cup.

Aren't we?

We get chances to make sure. Bobby slices a horrible shot well wide. *Oh Bobby*, I think, *that's not like you.* A minute later, Bally glides past Schnellinger, slips the ball inside to me and my shot's just as ugly. We want to finish this thing off, however the hell we can. Jack, receiving the ball in our half, experiments with dribbling it backwards towards Banksy. The crowd erupts in a thunder of boos. 'We want three!'

This is the untidiness of the endgame, when things can fall apart. Nobby unwisely attempts to clear with a bicycle kick, and misses. Beckenbauer tries to bully the game, to take it by the scruff of the neck. He wins a corner, which he drives in towards Mooro. Mooro can't clear or make the back pass to Banksy. Caught in possession he calmly dribbles out of the box and away towards the corner flag, holding off Weber until Martin pops up on the touchline and he nudges a little pass to him. Martin looks up and feeds Bally, who swivels inside then drills a superb defence-splitting pass to Roger in wide-open acres on the left. This is easily the move of the match. We are three on two, and could bury them here. I've pulled away to the right and Bobby is busting a gut to charge up and meet the pass laid on by Roger at the edge of the box. But it's just too much of a stretch and his shot – from his left foot when right would have been better – is flailed wide. This would have been the goal of the tournament. Bobby lies flat on his front. Overath, sportingly but also to hurry the game along, lifts him from the turf.

Not to be outdone, a minute later I produce probably the limpest shot of the match, if not my career.

We should try to calm down. There's a minute left. Play possession football, stop being greedy for glory. We're now seconds from the 39 steps.

The whistle goes. Big Jack, who's nine inches taller, has been judged to clamber all over little Seeler to head a bouncing ball. It's never a foul, and Nobby is the first to object with much snarling and gesturing. But he's in charge of the wall so back he comes to organise us. I'm surprised, all these decades later, to see myself in the wall as I have no memory of being there. Not that we are much use. Emmerich drills his shot straight past us. George blocks it. Held whips the ball across the goal, it ricochets off Schnellinger, pinballing into the path of Weber who slides in to hook the ball inside the post before Banksy or Ray can get there.

England 2 West Germany 2.

Mooro calls for handball and runs off to reason with the ref. I remember having no idea if the appeal was legitimate or just desperate. It doesn't matter because Herr Dienst has seen nothing amiss. With the benefit of hindsight he's plain wrong. In working on this book, I've looked at a lot of material and blow me down if one photograph doesn't capture the split second when the ball nestles quite clearly between Schnellinger's flank and his forearm. It looks as if he's holding it under his arm. And the referee has a perfect view.

So it wasn't a foul and it was a handball. In the 90th minute of the World Cup final, the Germans have got lucky. Very lucky.

Could it be England's turn next?

As Bobby, Roger and I line up back in the centre circle, all of us feeling punched in the gut, Schellinger trots past and kicks the ball from our feet. He's just got away with a match-saving handball and now he turns back and laughs, like the annoying kid in the playground. It's the game's only hint of niggling gamesmanship. I'd love to nip back in time and tell him that this is the last smile we'll see on his face today. But he'll find out soon enough.

And so to Alf's celebrated pep talk out on the pitch. He must have issued other instructions, tactical tips and so on, but no one in all the biographies and memoirs seems to have remembered them. All anyone knows is that he tells those of our team slumped on the grass – in the photographs, I can see it's Mooro and Jack – to stand up and not show the opposition they're tired. Look at the Germans, he says. They're finished. And then he tells us – in words that vary depending on who was recalling them – that we have won the thing in 90 minutes. Now we have to win it again in 30.

No one seems to listen more intently than Bally, whose socks are now down round his ankles. He hurries back to get on with the restart. Soon Mooro is clearing a cross into his path on the halfway line. With Schnellinger caught upfield, no one can get near him as he slaloms towards goal. His flying shot from outside the box dips towards Tilkowski, who palms it away for a corner.

This is to be the plot of extra time. Fatigue is setting in. Man-marking is getting ragged. Spaces are opening ever wider. Bally is everywhere. Schnellinger is nowhere. And Tilkowski is very busy. I challenge him for a high ball and he gets up limping. He pushes out a far-post drive from Bobby. A shot from Roger whistles past his post. Then in the 101st minute Tilkowski sends up a long high punt, which sails into our half. Jack watches the ball's descent, times his jump and skilfully targets his downward header towards the feet of Nobby alone in the centre circle.

Jack has just set up the most over-analysed goal in World Cup history. It's a wonder we ever heard the end of it.

The sun is out now and Nobby's shadow points him in the direction of the German goal. He glances up and sends that beautiful chip low over the head of Schnellinger towards the right-hand corner. Bally chases it down and whips his cross in. And there I am on the near post. The ball is arriving a bit to my right, away from the goal. It's awkward. If I'm going to shoot, I need to make a rapid adjustment. So with one touch of my right foot I both control the cross and steer the ball away from Schulz, who's looming behind me. I'm still in a tricky position. To get sufficient power into the shot, swivelling through 90 degrees from such a low position that I'm almost on my backside, takes all the skill I can muster. But I swing my right leg and, puffing out my cheeks, put force through the ball.

It flies past Tilkowski's hands, thuds against the underside of the bar, bounces down and I'm on the deck where I can see nothing.

Did it cross the line?

I've been debating this for 58 years. With the help of the linesman Bahramov, the referee Dienst makes his decision in 15 seconds. From the moment the ball hits the grass, that's how long it takes for them to reach a verdict. As they don't share a language, it's not as if they can have a richly fulfilling dialogue. Bahramov's nod is good enough for Dienst.

Roger is certain. Otherwise he'd follow up, not turn away. The ball bounces up so high that I'm not sure he'd get anywhere near it, but still. Instinct tells him it's a goal. That's always been good enough for me, and always will be.

Alternatively, you could put it this way: it was as much of a goal as West Germany's equaliser.

England 3 West Germany 2.

I want to add something now that I have never felt like saying in interviews or in front of audiences. And it is that I'm really proud of my technique. I hope this doesn't come over as conceited, but I've just scored not only my best-known goal, it's one of my best too. Control, twist, crouch, fire. Not easy! No one ever mentions this, but I'd like to put it out there now, for the record. Also, I want to say once and for all, and with a smile on my face, that I don't mind whether people think it's not a goal. In fact, I couldn't care less. I've loved talking about it all these years.

The camera captures me in close-up walking back for the kick-off. Then I break into a jog. The Germans are in such a hurry to restart that I'm still in the centre circle when play resumes.

In the second half of extra time, energy dies last in the youngest legs. Bally executes an outrageous backheel pass to Ray. Beckenbauer surges forward. Nobby shanks a cross and later admits to having no strength left. The Germans are by no means beaten, but we have more of the ball and when they get it they can't make any headway into the box. We are impregnable now. We've given them two silly goals. We won't give them another.

'Oh when the reds … go marching in,' sing the crowd.

Ray and George, Jack and Banksy are as calm as anything. Nobby successfully connects with a bicycle kick. Martin is an old head on young shoulders. Bally is still on fire. Bobby sprays passes. Roger keeps on running. So do I.

There's a minute to go. The crowd knows. Schulz, deep on the right, sends a hopeful ball towards the penalty spot. It lands on the mile-wide chest of Mooro, who looks like he's on a Sunday afternoon stroll as behind him Jack in his clearest Anglo-

Saxon instructs him to send the ball into outer space. That's not Mooro's style, though. Remember the best move of the match, started by Mooro down in the same corner? He has no desire to finish this performance with an ugly hoof. Possession is nine-tenths of the law. He looks up, spots Roger on a diagonal and casually tickles a pass to his feet. Roger catches the mood, traps it and at walking pace pushes it back. Mooro is now back near the corner flag. Jack must be having a coronary.

Meanwhile I'm on my own. The Germans have abandoned their positions. The camera cuts to Herr Dienst, who sends out mixed signals: he puts the whistle in his mouth and at the same time waves play on. I see this too. I know the game is over. I don't see people on the pitch, but I am certain that the day is ours. The thing now is to ensure the Germans never get another touch. Still there is no whistle. Mooro surges forward and lofts a pass from the gods 30 yards over three German heads. It bounces up to my chest to the left of the centre circle, then drops to my right foot. I turn from my shadow and head for goal. Bally, I'm vaguely aware, is off in space to my right and squealing for a pass. But I'm in just as good a position as him and have no other thought but to drive on. There's a defender to my right – is it Höttges? – but he's got half an eye on Bally. Behind me in my mind's eye I am aware of the pounding approach of Overath. But he's never going to get the ball off me, or even a touch on it. Later, I will try to claim that it doesn't matter where the shot ends up. As far away as possible will be fine. Outer space will do for Jack. A striker has instincts, though.

Here's Overath at my back. To shield the ball from him I cushion it across to my left foot. He can't stop me now. Only

Tilkowski can. I'm level with the penalty spot, and eyeing my shot when the ball hits a divot. It bobbles up just as I swing my left foot, which once upon a time I was patiently coached to use in our council house garden by my father now watching up in the stand. The bobble almost imperceptibly lifts the ball up from my instep and onto my laces where the hard bone of my foot imparts an extra measure of power.

I puff out my cheeks, let fly, and see the net billow.

England 4 West Germany 2.

Four for England. Three for Hurst. Head, right, left. A classical hattrick.

It's all over.

Bally gets to me first. Then Martin. Then the Charltons. The images of us celebrating will take their place in the nation's photo album. Bobby weeping, Jack praying, Nobby dancing, Ray and me finding the strength to hoist Mooro onto our shoulders as he brandishes the Jules Rimet trophy. All of us arm in arm, smiling into the future. One day in that future, though we don't know it yet, we will sell the medals in our hands and the shirts on our backs while holding on to our memories of today until half a dozen of us will lose those too.

But first, our squad mates come out to congratulate us. Among them is Jimmy, who's all smiles.

Now, we must form another line to meet the Queen. Here, though, is Alf, waiting for us beyond the edge of the grass, as full of joy as anyone will ever see him. He said England would win the World Cup and now, one by one, he thanks the men he chose to make it come true. He and Mooro embrace. It looks as if he wants to hug me also but I'm too dazed and weary to muster more than a knackered half-handshake. The man who picked me for this day clasps my left hand, then lets it drop as I, with my immortal teammates, follow our leader up the stairway.

Bobby Moore. Geoff Hurst. Bobby Charlton. Roger Hunt. Martin Peters. Jack Charlton. Ray Wilson. Alan Ball. George Cohen. Nobby Stiles. Gordon Banks.

Acknowledgements

I would like to thank three people without whom this book would not have been possible. Terry Baker, who also represents many other ex-footballers, has been my agent for over 20 years. But he is far more than that. He and his wife Freda run my stage show and have become great friends. Terry was instrumental in putting the idea of this memoir together, and it was him who selected my co-author.

I am also grateful to Jasper Rees for all the sterling work he has done, both in our many enjoyable meetings and in his diligent research, to help me piece together the story of 1966.

My greatest thanks go to my wife of 60 years. Judith has always kept away from the public eye and was initially reluctant to get involved in this venture. But it became clear that I could not tell the full story without her input, and she willingly came out of the shadows to play her part as an invaluable and generous collaborator. Apart from anything else, her memory for certain details of family life is much more reliable than mine!

I would also like to express my gratitude to all at Ebury Press, whose enthusiasm for this story is very much appreciated.

I am grateful to the Clementine Café in Cheltenham where the conversations that form the basis of this book took place over many a pot of tea.

My final thanks go to my teammates, who are with me in spirit, and to their wives who became our friends throughout so many happy reunions.

Bibliography

The following books and DVDs were useful reminders of 1966:

Banks, Gordon, *Banksy: My Autobiography* (Michael Joseph, 2002)

Charlton, Sir Bobby, with Lawton, James, *1966: My World Cup Story* (Yellow Jersey, 2016)

Charlton, Jack, *The Autobiography* (Partridge Press, 1996)

Cohen, George, with Lawton, James, *My Autobiography* (Greenwater, 2003)

Dickinson, Matt, *Bobby Moore: The Man in Full* (Yellow Jersey, 2014)

Hamilton, Duncan, *Answered Prayers: England and the 1966 World Cup* (Riverrun, 2023)

Hurst, Geoff, with Hart, Michael, *1966 and All That: My Autobiography* (Headline, 2001)

McColl, Graham, *England and the Alf Ramsey Years* (Chameleon, 1998)

Passingham, Ian, *66: The World Cup in Real Time* (Pitch, 2016)

Peters, Martin, with Hart, Michael, *The Ghost of '66* (Orion, 2006)

Rowlinson, John, *Boys of 66: The Unseen Story Behind England's World Cup Glory* (Virgin Books, 2016)

Stiles, Nobby, with Lawton, James, *After the Ball: My Autobiography* (Hodder & Stoughton, 2003)

Thomson, David, *4–2* (Bloomsbury, 1996)

Tossell, David, *Alan Ball: The Man in White Boots* (Hodder & Stoughton, 2017)

Tossell, David, *Natural: The Jimmy Greaves Story* (Pitch, 2019)

Wilson, Jonathan, *The Anatomy of England: A History in Ten Matches* (Orion Books, 2010)

Wilson, Jonathan, *Two Brothers: The Life and Times of Bobby and Jackie Charlton* (Little, Brown, 2022)

How England Won the World Cup '66: 40th Anniversary Edition (2006)

1966 FIFA World Cup Final in Colour (1966/2022)

Image Credits

Index

(GH indicates Geoff Hurst.)